PIGTAILS

&

STEEL

Andy McCall

Thanks again for everything. Hope our paths cross once again.

[signature]

Pigtails & Steel

In memory of my little girl, Penelope Claire. Daddy Loves You.

Pigtails & Steel

<u>Listen up, Dad</u>

Your wife or someone close to you probably bought you this because I know you didn't. You are more than likely just like I was and didn't need some book to tell me how to feel and how to live life every day. I didn't need another 12 steps or a "Thought of the Day". That just isn't me and half the time didn't have one thing to do with my situation. When they handed this to you, I'm sure you said, "Oh okay, thanks," and you really thought, "Great, another one."

I know you didn't Google "How to deal with _____" because nor did I at first. None of us wakes up and wants to read some daily devotional or self-help book to get us through the nightmare we are facing. We are looking for that answer and have thought about firing up the search engine and seeing if there was anything out there.

Truthfully, one day I did. I found nothing. There are hundreds of sayings, clichés, and books about grief. I didn't find one written by a dad who had been through what we have and told it like it was. I don't need 12 steps to a better me, 52 Bible verses that give me some glimmer of hope, or a new perspective on what is going on.

I'm a guy, and that's not how I roll. I've tried all those other things secretly and not a dang one of them work for more than an hour. I have had faith, lost it, found it again, and had it burn in flames all before eating breakfast. I'm right there with you, man. It sucks, and there is no way around it. You are either in a fight you cannot win or have already lost a part of your heart you will never get back. I get it. I've been there and stared at that same hospital wall you have.

I have walked those same halls too. I know how it feels to sit there in that doctor's office not being able to control anything. I know what it is like to leave the hospital at 4am to get to work after not sleeping. I know what it is like to watch them poke and prod your beautiful angel, then tell you they have no answers and have to do it all again the next day. There is nothing in life that prepares you for this. Nothing prepares you for being a man, a Dad, and a bystander in this situation. You feel defeated and helpless on a daily basis when you are supposed to be the rock, the one keeping it all together. I have been there and done that.

I'm still standing though. I still cry every day, even after more than a year ago. I go to work and provide for my wife and the family we hope to be. I am a man and that is what I'm supposed to do right? Throughout the book you'll realize I have only begun to work through my emotions, and I wish I had started much sooner. I'm not sugar coating anything. Life as we knew it before will never be again. There will be good days though; it isn't all dark and gloomy, so don't lose all hope.

The first few chapters of this book deal with things I wish I could talk to all you dads about. I don't know if there are any life altering ideas in there. That is for you to decide, but I do know I wish somebody would have talked to me about it. I didn't want the answers; I just wanted to hear that in some way, shape, or form that I could do this and it would end up being somewhat alright. I'm not here to tell you that "God gives strong people…blah blah blah" or "He won't give you more than you can handle." I've come to despise these sayings, and if I heard them once I've heard them a thousand times. You are strong, you can make it, and if you choose to believe in God, then I promise you He will help you through some very dark times. I'm not here to say I've worked it all out with the Man upstairs, but I am fortunate enough to have a stronger faith and feeling than I did before this whole rollercoaster began. I will leave it at that. I'm not here to preach or save you, but I do talk about it later, and it might make some sense in your situation.

If you are still reading this, then you know I am being completely honest. This book is not politically correct. It doesn't hold all the answers or some magic cure. This is just the story of a Dad like you who got the worst news of his life, lost his precious Penelope, and the shit show that ensued a year later.

INDEX

WAITING

END OF THE WEEK

PENELOPE'S PATH

I CAN'T PROTECT HER FROM THIS

ANGELS

MY LETTER TO CANCER

I DON'T KNOW WHAT TO SAY

FACEBOOK AND FUNDRAISERS

MY FAVORITE THING

THE DANCE

"SHE LOOKS SO GOOD?!"

GOOGLE SAYS SORRY, NO RESULTS FOUND

TWO PARENTING RULES

TWO HEADED MONSTER

SWEET P'S SERVICE

BREAKING BEANS

1ST FATHER'S DAY WITHOUT P

4TH AND 1

THE POWER OF NICE

HOW TO GRIEVE

HOW ARE YOU?

DEEP IN THE TIMELINE

TO MY BOYS

NOTHING MORE WAS NEEDED…

Pigtails & Steel

OUR STORY, YOUR STORY, EVERYONE HAS A STORY

Everybody has a story. Everyone is going through something. I'm sure there are parts of your story that make parts of mine seem like a breeze. That was the whole idea about putting all this together. Nobody in our situation wants to read about some story that ended up like a fairy tale or about how they made lemonade out of lemons. I'm over here making pints of beer go empty if I'm doing anything. Truthfully, this is the last chapter that I wrote for this book. It isn't because it is the end, but it was the beginning of life as I know it now. I didn't want to relive part of this, and I cried as much writing this as I did the rest of the entire book.

The last thing you want to hear about is another sad story about a beautiful, little girl. If you are like me, behind the rough, manly exterior is a softer side that just about can't take seeing another kid suffer. You see it in your own life, and that right there is all you can handle. I'm not going to into every single detail about every appointment, but I also want you to know the reason I've been writing all this time.

Pigtails & Steel

This chapter isn't like one of those puppy commercials telling you a sad story. I'm also not throwing it all out there for some type of Super Parent award for what Ellen and I went through. Our story is just that, a story. It was our hand that was dealt, and although a completely crappy hand, we made the best out of it and shared our little Sweet P with the world for her short time.

Penelope was born on July 11, 2014, as a happy and healthy baby girl. She was our little miracle as we conceived her through in vitro fertilization (IVF). Our little princess had a great three months, then we noticed some things out of the ordinary. She started having seizures, and at four months, she began having leg twitches. She then started having spasms that caused her arms to flail out and her eyes to roll back in her head. Those turned into clusters, and they began getting longer and more frequent. That was when we took her to Knoxville. Standing in the middle of that exam room my world first stopped. The neurologist diagnosed my baby girl with infantile spasms, and the look on her face as she told me is one I will never forget. I say this was when the world stopped, but the hospital visits started. If it was rare or severe, Penelope was going to get it. She had surgeries for her constant UTI's and even wore a half body cast that put us in the hospital until Christmas Day due to a tight hip muscle.

She was diagnosed with two rare diseases after that. The first one was Polymicrogyria and the second, Aicardi syndrome. I said severe earlier, but I should have said rare. We don't believe the Aicardi syndrome was right, and in our continuous search for more answers, have found a group of beautiful children that could be her twins, as they possess many of the same afflictions associated with a syndrome. Penelope more than likely had Schintzel Giedion syndrome, but we will likely never know because what is even harder than getting a geneticist to give you answers when you need them is trying to get answers after your child has passed and you need help. My daughter's diagnoses effects less than 5,000 people worldwide and is associated with a very short life expectancy. I could go into detail about all that came with it, but there is no need in that. Her diagnosis was not her definition. It was just a name that described part of what made up her insides, and that's all we will ever worry about it.

We thought we had a grip on the situation, but we should have known better, right? The next little bit was something I never even imagined on my worst day. It had nothing to do with surgeries or doctor's visits. It had nothing to do with tube feedings or medicine schedules. It wasn't even the sleepless nights or hospital stays. We were sitting on the couch one day and noticed that she wasn't using her legs. They were as limp as they once were strong. Penelope didn't do a whole lot physically, but she would kick those legs like nobody's business. There was no kicking at all, not even a reaction when I squeezed her little toes. Something was very wrong.

We took her to the emergency room, and they did some tests and a brain and spine MRI. When we didn't get an answer right away, I went back to work that morning. When my phone rang and I heard Ellen crying, I knew it wasn't good, but I never expected to hear the word cancer come through the speaker. To this day, I'll never forget what that sounded like.

Luckily, our home hospital has a St. Jude affiliate in the 1st floor, and we did not have to wait a second for what was next. We were referred to St. Jude's in Memphis with a quick stop at their children's hospital for a biopsy before they could figure out exactly what was wrong. Ellen flew with Penelope, and I drove all through the night after getting our affairs in order quicker than I could even think.

The results came back, and she was diagnosed with Stage 4 medulloepithelioma. It was so aggressive that the tumor in her brain had grown from the time she left Johnson City to the MRI in Memphis.

There was no cure, and there was no way that my little girl would beat this. I couldn't do anything for her to fix this. They gave her weeks to months to live at most. Dr. A gave us three options: intense chemo, do nothing, or try a low dose oral chemotherapy and head home. Obviously, we loaded the car and headed back home. She spent her life in hospitals; she was going to finish this journey at home.

We spent every second giving her the best life we could. We made her a bucket list that included things like ride a motorcycle with her Uncle, take a Jeep ride, dye her hair pink, and with the help of some amazing people, we even got to take her to the beach and stick her toes in the ocean. I'll never be able to fully thank those special people that made that happen- it was truly a miracle. We even made a special friend in Destin, Florida, who did everything in his power to make sure that she had the best experience possible.

We had more plans but noticed that morning at the beach she wasn't feeling very well, and it was time to go back. We made it all the way home and after a good night's sleep, we knew it was time. On June 9, 2016, Penelope did not have to hurt anymore. She is now in Heaven, picking flowers and running around with all those little kids just like her. She visits us every day, and I feel her with me all the time. Her body might be gone, but her spirit and name will live forever.

She got to do more things in 23 months than most kids ever get to do in a lifetime. She made it to the top of the world at Logan Pass in Glacier National Park with her Auntie Amy, Rory, and Bennett. She tasted barbeque in a basement restaurant in Memphis after going to the top of the pyramid on the banks of the Mississippi River. Penelope sat on her mother's hip as the Governor of

Pigtails & Steel

Tennessee signed the CBD Bill that legalized the use of CBD Oil for children all across the state of Tennessee. She attended all the meetings with her best friend Josie as they showed what legalizing cannabis can do to help stop seizures. We did not let "what was wrong" stop us from doing all those things a little girl should do. I am proud to say that Penelope Claire McCall left her mark on this world. She was little, but she was fierce.

Pigtails & Steel

PART 1

These first few chapters are simply different sections of your life as you know it. They are important parts you need to recognize and really think about. I'm not going to start in on your personal life or finances. That part for me is still a never-ending battle of being occasionally right and occasionally broke. There are many other topics in this situation, but then it turns into some self-help type book that you and I both are going to throw in the corner and hope we can re-gift at a white elephant Christmas party. Hopefully, through this, you will see that you are not alone in whatever your journey is. I pride myself in being a strong, independent man who can provide for his family. That doesn't mean I'm not a mess inside or that I had any clue how to deal with all this. There are new things that pop up every day that I'm still trying to figure out, but these, I can assure you, will be present in everyone's journey.

<u>PLEDGE ALLEGIANCE TO THE STRUGGLE</u>

7:13 a.m.

3 day old khakis, but no stains yet thank the Lord.

Half wrinkled shirt, but the front looks ok.

Extra-large cup of coffee.

Some random hip hop station playing louder than it should, just to wake you up.

Pledge Allegiance to the Struggle.

This is what people see first thing in the morning. What they don't see is that you spent the last 14 hours sitting in the ICU with your little girl and wife. They don't see that you woke up at 5 am after a few hours of sleep to drive home, get a shower, check the bills, pet the cat, and start your day all over again. They don't see the burden you carry of leaving your little girl in a hospital bed, not knowing what news today's doctors will bring.

Today will be a struggle. People all day who know your situation will ask how it's going, but you know as well as I do, they don't want to hear the real answer. All day you will have to listen to how tired or how sore someone is because they didn't sleep right or stayed up watching Netflix all night. You want to ask them if they know how it feels to sleep on a recliner and wake up every hour to a nurse taking some sort of vitals, but you don't; you just nod your head and give them the sympathy they want. Last but not least, you'll get to hear the 99 problems of your coworkers that are so trivial or superficial that you want to hand them a catheter and syringes full of antibiotics and say, "Here, my 19-month-old daughter in the hospital needs you to catheterize her and push these down her throat while she screams." But you don't. You just listen and give them the comfort they need. You do all this because you are a special needs Dad, and you are special too.

Special needs Dads are a different breed. I have to remind myself sometimes that I'm doing the best I can, and that's good enough. There is no doubt in my mind if people saw what was going through our head's in a day, they'd send us to the nearest mental health facility. We might not be physically in that hospital, therapy appointments, or at home working on head control and sitting up, but mentally we have never left those places. We might be sitting in a business meeting or teaching kids geometry, but our minds are constantly fighting the battle of "Can I do this" and "Am I good enough?"

Yes, you are, and yes, you can. No matter what the struggle is today, you will make it. Don't worry about the struggles of tomorrow, or you might miss a miracle or at least progress from today. There are 400 clichés', but you have to find what works for you and go with it. Whether it is an extra-large cup of coffee, a bible verse, a CD of old school rap, or even a picture of your little one on a good day; you use that and never let it go. Life is a struggle, and it seems like it might never get better.

That's all it is, a struggle, but you have to remind yourself it isn't the end.

DAILY LIFE

First off, let's be real. There is nothing daily about it. Living this life of having a child with special needs, or, as I'm living thereafter, you are wishing it could be about the daily grind. You truthfully are living in sections: breakfast, med time, appointment time, and everything in between. In the hospital, you are living in hours and sometimes minutes. Every situation is different and on a different schedule. I don't use one of those wall calendars, but if I did, I'm pretty sure I would buy stock in Post-It Notes and colored Sharpies.

I don't know what you are going through, but I do know this. There are certain things you need to accomplish every day. You are probably thinking I'm going to tell you to take time for yourself and so on. Well, I am. I'm not going to do it in the way you are thinking. You don't have time for meditation and certainly not time for a nap every day. You have probably forgotten what a nap is by this time in your life.

I had to consciously make myself think about me. That sounds weird I know. Whether it was the 5 am drives back home before work or the nightly drives back to the hospital. It could have been the 30 minutes I was waiting on her to get an MRI or even the most special moments she was asleep on my shoulder drooling away. I had to remember to think about me.

Did I eat enough today? Did I even eat? Did I drink something other than coffee?

Those were normal questions, but I started to make myself think about my life each day differently. Did I laugh or at least attempt to laugh? Did I focus on anything good that happened versus all the bad shit that went on? Did I tell that nurse thank you? Was there a moment today that no sickness or cancer could ever take away?

I didn't want to forget these things. I made myself go back and actually make these things happen. There's a whole lot of time to be the sad Dad, but I wasn't letting cancer have that part of my life too. So what if we couldn't move more than two feet from the monitors, we were still going to read a book. I don't know if she even woke up because of those meds, but I still danced with her in the rain. She might not have felt good at all, but by God we were driving to the ocean and sticking her feet in it.

Daily life became a question of what I could focus on that didn't make life seem so bad. I'm not telling you what to do or acting like I'm the perfect hospital Dad. There were numerous nights of my aimlessly scrolling through Facebook, crying, cussing, and watching the monitor. I just chose to do something different, and it helped. Many nights in the hospital were spent crying, but I can promise you the ones we played in the pudding and watched cartoons together pop in my mind a whole lot more.

DOCTORS AND THEIR BOSSES: THE NURSES

You've seen more doctors, specialists, and nurses than you have normal people when you live in and out of hospitals. You have had good ones, smart ones, weird ones, young ones, old ones, and all that falls in between. There are times you have no idea what they are talking about, and others you feel you know more about the situation than they do. Both situations are okay, I promise.

When you have a child who is sick, you feel as if you have had a crash course in med school whether you wanted it or not. You know how to silence the monitors, dispense meds, and can even diagnose what is wrong faster than the ER staff. You know your child better than anyone with some degree or a white coat, but you have to remember they are doing their best and that they are humans too.

I can't tell you how many times I've said, "That doctor had better get their butt in here now or I'm going to lose it!" I've said about a million times, "Where in the hell is that nurse, my daughter needs her meds." You are probably right there with me. It is very easy to get frustrated and take it out on those nurses who are in and out all hours of the night. They are just doing their job, and, believe me, they are the ones you want on your side. They are the real bosses. They are the ones who get it done. They might not be signing the bottom of the discharge papers, but they are the ones who get the papers to you quick. They are the ones stressing just as much as you are about why the meds aren't working. They hold back the tears in front of you, but I've rode many an elevator with a nurse getting off shift who couldn't hold it back anymore.

I'm only writing this because you need help in these situations, and some of these nurses are your voice. Penelope had this one nurse, Nurse K, whom we called, "Her Nurse." We lived in and out of our local children's hospital, and at first it was just coincidence that she was her nurse. Over time, Penelope was her little girl on the 2nd floor, and that's just how it was. Nurse K became almost like family because she cared as much about Miss P as we did. I look back now, and I don't know if I would have stayed sane if it wasn't for knowing she was taking care of her while I was at work and couldn't be there. As many times as she woke me up on that little couch, she also gave me rest knowing P was in good hands. I knew Nurse K would do anything in her power to make her better. This is what you need to look for in that hospital room. The positives are there; just sift through all the blood draws and beeping and you'll find them wearing badges and a smile.

I did come to love a few of her doctors beyond them taking care of Penelope. Dr. S was her urologist and saw her about as many times as anyone did. He always gave it to us straight and did everything he could for P when she was with him. I felt like whatever he said was the right thing to do, and I never questioned him. When we got the news we were going to St. Jude's, I called his office and although he wasn't there, they would let him know. It wasn't an hour later I got a call from him as he was walking out of a conference in California and wanted to know what he could do and if we or St. Jude's needed him to call his cell no matter the time. The letter he wrote us when Penelope passed is still hanging on our wall.

They say St. Jude's is a special place, and all I can say is special doesn't even begin to describe it. You never want to have to be a family there, but if you do find yourself in those circumstances, you will be glad a place like that exists. All the people- from the cleaning ladies to the specialists- were top notch, including Dr. A. He was the man who told me he had no answers, but also the man I saw and understood true passion and care from. It was in his eyes I saw what it meant to be a doctor who cared about children more than anything in the world. He was a shining light for us in during our darkest times. I'll never forget his prayer during our last meeting or the words of encouragement in emails as we stayed in touch. There are special people in this world, and Dr. A is at the top of the list in my books.

You'll come across doctors and nurses you will like and dislike. As a dad, you have every right and must speak up about what your little one needs. There will be doctors you think can do more and some who might be a little over the top with another two days stay. Just remember there will be nurses like Nurse K and ones like Nurse P who will braid her hair to make her look so beautiful even when she's feeling so bad. Speak up, listen, and go with the flow in that little room. Do your best to be the best Dad you can be, but a friend in scrubs never hurt anything. I can promise you that.

YOU MIGHT NEED TO SHOOT SOMETHING

Like I've said, I haven't figured out all the answers to this messed up life, but I do know one thing that is true: you have to find an outlet to get all these emotions out. I tried living with it all bottled in, and I became one of the saddest, dejected, and, if you ask my wife on occasion, the biggest asshole on the planet. You have to find something that takes you away from all this mess and gives you a way to decompress. If you don't, you will regret it and not be the best person you can be for yourself and your family. That old quote "You can't pour from an empty cup" is very true whether you want to believe it or not.

I chose two things: writing and weightlifting. I've always lifted weights from high school to playing college football and real heavy during the "has been" years. Those first few years required me to do it, the latter years I required myself to do it. I noticed though while I was bouncing 315 off my chest, I was still thinking about her. I was thinking about money, insurance, medicine, and everything else but lifting weights. I enjoyed going to the gym and getting a good one in with my friends, but it still wasn't enough. I was still burdened by everything inside of me. The shit show wasn't leaving my body with the sweat I left on the bench like I had hoped it would. I'm sure you are seeing a comparison with those walks that your nurses, wife, or doctors tell you to go take when they see you are stressed. Yes, it is great to get some fresh air, but it just changes the scenery for your worries you are trying to hide. I needed something more, something different.

I started writing. I've always been able to write things like essays or football banquet speeches but never have written for fun. If I did write for fun, I sure wasn't telling my friends in football or at the gym. I wasn't going to set myself up for that roasting session, hell no.

It wasn't until I created the blog and hit submit on the first one that I realized this was it for me. That feeling didn't last an hour; it lasted all the way to the next big demoralizing blow that life delivered me. All that mess that was inside my brain finally came out, and it felt good. I didn't even care that nobody other than my wife and Mom would probably read it. I found my out. I found a way to deal with it.

To this day, I have never read what are in these next chapters. I don't need to. I lived it. I got it out of my head, and that is where it needs to stay.

I'm not saying that you need to write and follow in my footsteps. I'm saying you need to find what works for you and do it. Don't care what anybody thinks. You don't even have to tell anyone else if you don't want to. I chose to put 200 words on a page; you might need to put 200 shells into a target. Every time you pull the trigger, just yell whatever you are pissed about. It could be painting, building, heck, I don't know. You do you and be good with that. I just believe with all my heart that you have to find something. Being a man and dealing with these burdens can ruin you. Being strong means taking care of yourself as much as it does taking care of those around you.

THREE PREACHERS

Spirituality is a big theme in this life we live. I don't know what your feelings are about God, and I don't think it is any of my business to know. I don't proclaim to be a very religious person, but I do say that I am a very spiritual person after going through all this. I hope that before reading this you have found something to believe in and that your faith is strong. I hope that for you. If you are like me though, it wavers every single day, and I am grasping at air trying to figure it all out. I heard something one time that made me feel ok with not walking back into my church in over a year.

"I'd rather be at home thinking about God than at church thinking about home."

I do believe though that in this journey we are taking you have to find three preachers. It takes all three and their way of thinking to make you feel comfortable in your own spirituality. Again, I'm not talking religion; I'm talking about believing in something bigger than us, bigger than what is going on here and trying to make some sort of sense about it. Find yourself an old school, a new school, and a truth. They are there. You just have to look for them. They all three have different traits that I believe help us figure this thing out.

Old School:

He has been around my family and me for a long time. He is the pastor at my church, he married Ellen and I, and he was at the hospital every time we were there for an extended amount of time. He never failed. He was always there, sometimes just to check in and other times to see what we needed. He always asked about us as much as Penelope and ended our time together with a prayer from the heart. You need somebody like this. They are always there, and it makes you feel comfortable in a way you don't understand at first. Look for that person. I guarantee if you think about it you will find that old school consistency that you might not think you need, but you really do.

New School:

There will be somebody that shows up in your time of need that knows what you are going through and has the exact right words to say at the exact right time.

It freaked me out the first couple of times I won't lie. I'm thinking to myself, "This dude is in my head, and there's no way in hell he knew I was feeling like this."

There was a guy who has a child with special needs and is one of the Godliest men I have ever met. Whatever the situation was, the words flowed from his mouth like they were coming from the Big Man himself. It was so weird sometimes that even when I didn't want to talk to him due to being tired or just plain over it all, he helped me through that situation with something that gave me hope. There is somebody there for you that just gets it and when all else fails is your safety net. Look for that person. It doesn't have to be all about God's word, but it is all about that genuine care for another human being. It could be magic. I just called it his time.

Pigtails & Steel

The Truth:

I say you need three people because although consistency and a little bit of "genuine magic" can still leave a little doubt, sometimes you just need it as straight as a shot of Jack. That is where a man like "The Truth" comes in. I could write a few chapters about our times together, and I'm sure he could write a few on me. I tried to think about God and our situation and put it in His hands, but I wasn't always so sure. I was far from sure when I rolled into Memphis after being told my daughter has Stage 4 cancer. To heck with "A Plan," I needed something real. He didn't feed me scripture or things I wanted to hear. He sat me down like a man, gave me some things to think about, prayed for my strength as the Father in this situation, and proceeded to say we needed to get a beer and catch up. He hadn't seen me in almost 12 years, but he knew as a man I needed it straight and needed to make my own mind up right then and there. Doubt causes only confusion, and I had all the answers within me from my raising. I just needed to straighten them out and do what I thought was best.

As a man, a father, and a husband, we need consistency, timing, and a straight shot. Living like we are doesn't leave much room for "What ifs" and "Well, maybes." I also don't think these three people in your life have to do solely with your faith and religion. They can be anybody during your journey in this time of need. These three just happened to help me out with the hardest part of all this: faith and belief. There were many others along the way who dropped a whole lot of knowledge that helped form my thoughts on the subject, and I appreciate them too.

I'll leave you with this thought: I don't care what you believe in, but believe in something. Believe it with all your heart and go with it. Take in all that is coming at you and absorb it into your own way of dealing with it. Yes, I still cuss at the sky and ask why He took her and not me. Yes, I still don't 100 percent believe that it is all part of a "plan." And yes, I still have not walked back into the church since her funeral. That's all ok though. It's me and my beliefs, and I stand by them. Just like you should stand by yours.

Pigtails & Steel

Part 2: MY LIFE, MY BLOG

This next section contains my thoughts, word for word, in the order that my life unfolded. I still to this day have never read a word of what is in your hands. I have never gone back and looked at what I wrote. I took it out of my head and onto the keyboard and never looked back. I wrote some of these in hospital rooms, at home, and even laying in my grandmother's floor. I wrote it when I needed to get it out of my head and that is where it will stay. These pages represent all that I went through and most times couldn't express to anyone other than Ellen, and now, for whatever it's worth, I'm sharing them with you.

THE BEGINNING

Monday May 2nd is a day I will never forget. I went home
that night before to get some rest. I am a 2nd grade teacher and a high
school football coach, so some sort of sleep is vital. As good as it
sounds to get a good night's rest, I hate every second of being away
from my little girl and Ellen who are in the hospital, but that's for
another talk. I knew we were going to get some kind of news that
day, but I never expected someone to tell us it was a highly aggressive
cancer. That thought never entered my mind.

Ellen called me from the hospital, and as soon as I heard her start
talking, my world stopped. I went to another room in school to be
alone, but it wouldn't have mattered if I was in Times Square;
everything stopped, everything went silent. I literally spent the next
couple minutes after hanging up the phone standing there numb. I
couldn't cry, I couldn't think, I couldn't even process it all. I went
from sad to mad and 400 emotions in between in the time it took me
to tell my Principal and my team that I had to go and get to my girls.

I'm only going to write about this journey because I have a
hard time getting it all out. There's only a handful of people who

understand to a degree what this life inside my head is like. I'm going

to cuss, I'm probably crying while I write some of this. I'll probably

say things that people don't agree with, things you won't understand,

but truthfully, I could care less. Penelope always tells me how it is, so

I figure I can too.

4 WALLS

You want to get really in touch with your thoughts and feelings? Sit in a freaking hospital room for more than one day. You want to start getting delirious and questioning everything you know? Sit in a hospital room for more than three days. People always ask, "How are you doing?" Well, you probably don't want to know the truth, so I hit you with the "I'm ok."

I get so pissed when somebody says, "I'm Tired!" or "I have so much going on I can't handle it." Usually it is because they watched Netflix all night or they don't do their damn job and leave everything to the last minute. I'll rant more about that later, but that has to do with the shit-storm of emotions that are in my head on a daily basis. One of my coworkers said it best: "You just have to act like you are in a movie and be the best actor you can." I scream WTF internally about 20 times a day, and that's not towards kids. My kids are my escape. They make me happy.

Truthfully, I don't see how Ellen stays sane having to stay when I go to work. I've seen a lot of hospital walls over the past couple years, and they all bring the same emotions. I start out scared

44

for my little girl and what the results will show. Then I get anxious while they fiddle fart around trying to make arrangements for what is next. Usually it will take too long, and I get mad and start cussing under my breath. Next, I will get a little relief because they start making her feel better. From that point, it usually is a roller coaster of all those and about 10 more combined.

Sure you can get out, walk around, and people watch, but you still have to come back to these walls. You sit there and memorize every poster, every medical procedure, every nook and cranny just trying to find something different that takes your mind off of that little girl laying in the bed in the middle of the room.

Cell phones and Clash of Clans makes it easy to mindlessly wander for a few minutes, but if that Wi-Fi is shitty, then you are going to have a bad time. I don't mind reading. I've actually finished a few books sitting in these recliners, but with so many people coming in and out, it's hard to get a good read.

Distractions aside, hospital stays make me crazy as hell. I start diagnosing P's illness and make it a hundred times worse than it ever is. I usually start judging and guessing about the nurses that come in and out and the doctors who make their rounds. It's always funny to see the residents who look like they've been on 3 day bingers. I don't trust a word they say.

My emotions are just that: Mine. Other than Ellen and my friend Logan, it is hard for anybody to understand what's up in my head. The rage is the hardest part to control, and how I've gone this long without my fist going through something or someone is beyond me. I'm really good at keeping all these thoughts and emotions in. It's best for everybody.

THERE'S NO CRYING IN BASEBALL

I don't even like crying in general. It messes up my contacts or makes my glasses fog for one. That is just the first thing that makes me upset about crying.

Ellen is the only person I think I can even cry in front of and not feel weird about it. I feel weird crying to my Mom even. It has nothing to do with not feeling comfortable or feeling like I can't, but that's just me. I'm sure there is some deep seeded "thing" inside of me that a therapist with an uncomfortable couch could elaborate on, but I'm not at that point yet.

I don't cry when we lose a game. I don't cry at the end of a season. I think that is just weird. If you lost a game, you obviously didn't do something well enough. When the season is over, I'm just happy I got to be a part of it, and, yeah, it sucks it's over, but the sun is still going to come out in the morning.

I cried when my friends Chase and Michael died. Those were the first times I felt helpless, but I had forgotten what that felt like. I don't cry a whole lot when bad stuff happens to me. When it comes to my daughter though, there's a different type of cry that

47

happens, and it only happens with her. That feeling about makes me sick to my stomach, and I just get mad again. When I get news about P, I always make sure I'm somewhere alone because I can't hold it back. It never fails- I cry. Most of the time I don't let Ellen see me cry, but then there's times I send her the "Cried all the way home, FML" text which is code for I got home and am Ok now.

For me, my crying spot is in the bathroom. I think it is because I can look in the mirror about halfway through and tell myself to quit being a pansy and get it together. My lifting partner right before he's about to do something heavy says, "alright you big baby let's go." I don't know if he means to say it, but it's a mild version of what I tell myself when I'm crying, and I always think of those moments (random I know). I know it is good to cry, but, sweet Lord, it sucks. I like to cuss a lot when I get done crying. Maybe that is my way of cleansing everything. I'm just glad nobody hears me. I mean I say some messed up stuff. I think I have made up a few new ones that would make Bobby Knight proud, but Coach B disappointed at the same time.

Pigtails & Steel

It's almost like crying is just a precursor to me getting mad as hell. I don't know if other people get that way, but I don't know any other way.

I've cried more in the past week than I have in my entire life I think. I don't think crying is a sign of weakness or any crap like that; I just don't like it. Maybe one day I'll think differently about it. As for now, I'll just stick to crying in the bathroom, cussing the mirror, and walking back out like nothing is wrong.

BIG GUY IN A LITTLE CHAIR

1 a.m.

Sitting next to a hospital crib in a chair that is made for someone half my size. Ellen is trying to get some sleep, but Little Bit has other plans. She's a tough one, but she doesn't handle the pain of surgery real well. So that means Dad gets to sit here, watch the final season of Dexter, and think about random stuff.

I hate fake people. I love seeing the smiles on a kid's face when they make me a drawing or picture for P. I can't stand listening to people talk about college football and the players making bad decisions. All they do is criticize them, but they have no idea what they go through daily. I really wish I got to learn more from one of the smartest men I know, my friend Jason, but he still teaches me whether he knows it or not. I think burritos or wraps are the best form of lunch. I take two scoops of pre-workout, but I know my heart probably hates me when I do. I wish I was sitting in the back yard watching our dog, Tink, smell the grass for the scent of cats and deer. I miss eating breakfast with my Pop every Saturday.

These are the random things that go through my mind at 1 am in a tiny chair.

I understand people have issues, especially if I meet you in a hospital. But do you have to be so damn rude? It blows my mind how incredibly insensitive other people are when in public. The cafeteria is like the watering hole of the Serengeti. Why can't we just be nice and smile to each other. You are going to get your dang double heart attack patty with extra cheese, but just be nice about it.

Entitled youth. I'm probably going to write a two pager on this one later, but it gets harder and harder to bite my tongue. I don't look any farther than the parents, or the lack thereof, to see why that little shit is the way they are. It's getting bad in the world, and I don't think it is going to get better.

Why do people look down on janitors? Don't act like you never have. I won't lie, I used to avoid a janitor or not say much to them, but I changed that in college. I have had some of the best conversations with janitors whether they be at school, hospitals, or anywhere really. They see and hear everything. Just remember that.

Pigtails & Steel

I love beer and I can't stand people who judge others who drink in public. If I want to have a beer with my friends at 5 pm at the local upscale bar I'm going to do it. So what if I teach your kid. They might be the reason I'm having that beer. I have never once in my life let my extracurricular activities affect anything in my life. I graduated at the top of my class in high school, college, and for my Masters degree. I also put some microbrewer's kid through college probably. Don't judge me differently because I like to have a beer or six every now and then.

I can't stand people who chew with their mouths open. Maybe that is the teacher in me, but it irks me.

I have a hard time shutting my brain down at night. All I want to do is heal Penelope. All I want to do is take her pain away. Since I can't, I fill my brain with some random stuff to keep me thinking and keep me busy.

BEEP BEEP F'ING BEEP

There's no sleep in a hospital. We all know that. The biggest thing that limits that sleep, other than residents with no bedside manner, is that freaking monitor.

Technology is great, but it is also inaccurate at times. A lot of times. Before I write this, yes, nurses, I know that there is a privacy button, and I know how to use it. The thing is, other than with our couple awesome nurses, they don't really like you to hit it. So constantly, just as my mind drifts from the hell we are living in, I get reminded of it with a series of beeps that don't mean shit. Some little red node might have moved a millimeter the wrong way and now says she either has no pulse or she isn't breathing. That in turn sends you into a millisecond panic because you fear that it is true. Oh wait, nope, she just yawned, and it moved again. FML. So I go back to playing my mindless game on the iPad and just as I hit a new level- BEEP BEEP BEEP BEEP BEEP. Oh look, right after my panic attack subsides, I notice P has fallen asleep again, and it now says, she's breathing too slowly. It never fails that someone has to rush in, mess with her, wake her up, and then we start this process all over again. Repeat this every hour on the hour for 24 hours.

I get it really. This will come in handy if something really happens. After surgery I believe it to be a necessity; after that I'm not so sure. I would still pick the lesser of two evils and let me watch my daughter and be her alarm. I think my football voice of "Somebody get the hell in here and save my daughter!" would work just as well as ole girl at the nurses station checking Facebook instead of the monitors.

No matter how much I rant and rave, I will still BEEP BEEP BEEP get interrupted by that little tan box of jackass just as I fall asleep.

SPROUT AND MY SANITY

P doesn't really watch and focus in on a lot of things, but she seems to notice things on Sprout tv more than others. Slowly, I'm trying to get her into "Rugrats" and the good stuff, but until then it will stay on "Sprout".

First, let's talk about the actual people on there. It takes a special breed of weird to be that happy and demonstrative with your facial expressions all the time, especially when you are working with a chicken and a talking star. Pre-K teachers are that type of breed. I respect them 100%, but there's no way in hell I could do that. My buddies and I talked one time about them being not bad looking at all, but when all you get to stare at are cartoons, you find anything more attractive. They do have a pretty chill job though. All you have to do is wear pajama pants and act like a 3-year-old. Not too stressful. They throw in some Spanish every now and then, but maybe that's just their way of appealing to their Mexican dealer's kids who supply them with Happy Pills. Either way, that would just be a weird job that I don't think I could do day in and day out.

"Chica"

Chica knows a little too much about how potty training is fun and makes some pretty serious diet decisions for my liking. That squeak makes me want to rip my ears out, but maybe that is why she's on first thing in the morning. Let's wake everybody up with the most annoying sound we can.

"Caillou"

Caillou doesn't deserve a paragraph. That little shit is on the same level of giving everybody trophies.

The "Berenstain Bears" are the exact opposite of Caillou. They are the definition of cartoon and should be a staple of every childhood. The books are at the top of my list. I could go on and on, but I rank them up there with the original Teenage Mutant Ninja Turtles.

The "Floogals" are creepy as well. They have four ears, They are a bunch of different colors. To be from a different planet they are pretty dumb. If they say Whoman instead of Human once, they say it 500 times in 30 minutes. Their daily projects do teach kids about common things in life, but I think a good question from a kid of "What's that?" would do the same and be better than watching this junk.

"Superwings", "Sydney Sailboat", and "Astroblast"- I have no problem with. The episodes really aren't that bad and they have some funny stuff on there. Maybe I'm delirious by that point, who knows.

"Maya the Bee" is a creepy one as well. I don't mind the theme song, and P really likes this one, but has anybody noticed that Maya's best friend is a dung beetle? I know the kids don't get it, but just about every episode somebody is rolling in crap. The dung ball race episode was the best. I mean who doesn't like a good ball of poop rolling around the forest with all your friends. The focus on perfecting the roundness of the poop for optimal rolling really took some writing genius. I could imagine my friends getting wasted and writing this. Maya is smart though and usually figures out her problems, which is ok with me. At least she isn't crying to Mommy like Caillou when it starts to rain or something.

"Ruff Ruff, Tweet, and Dave" is interactive and other than pausing for too long that makes me impatient, I like it. Dave is a lot like me. He's bigger than the other kids and doesn't care to let them know about it. He also falls asleep first. I like his style.

So if you haven't noticed by now. Ellen is asleep and P is resting, which means I'm going out of my mind and talking about Sprout. I don't know if this qualifies me for a straight jacket or not, but it sure seems like it. So Caillou, I hope you grow up without friends and, yes, it is Dave. It's always Dave.

ENTERING THE GATES

Emotional would be an understatement. Driving in the gates at St. Jude's will just about take your breath away. It's like entering a place that you are happy exists, but don't want to ever step foot in. I've always known or heard that St. Jude's is an emotional rollercoaster, but I must be unstrapped on an upside down ride going backwards. Externally, I am ok. Internally, I'm so fucked up I can't even put it into words; that's why I cuss I guess. Ellen cried first, so she gets the prize, but every time I'm alone with P or away from them for a few seconds, I about can't hold it back.

Everybody here is so nice. You ask. They do. You ask a dumb question; they smile and make you feel better about it. Hell, even a delivery guy showed us where one of the offices was like it was his job to serve us. I know it is part of their training, to be so uplifting, but they've aced that part for sure.

The ladies at the front desk have everything covered, and the ladies at registration have everything down to an exact science. When you walk into the clinic, everything is laid out ready for you like you are the only person who matters at the moment. The lady at the pharmacy the other day was rocking out to Michael Jackson, taking my paper, and acting like she wasn't in a place full of sadness.

I don't like being here one bit. I don't want to think about what happens next week when we meet with doctors. I don't want to watch my little girl undergo anything else. But like the people here at St. Jude, I will smile, I will do what is asked of me and go about our business.

THE EYES ABOVE THE MASK

Two little girls broke my heart on Saturday May 14, 2016. Neither of them was my girl. I have no idea who they are or what their names are. I don't know where they are from or if I will ever see them again, yet strangely, I feel like I know them on a different level. I feel like I should be there holding their hands right now.

Both girls were in wheelchairs with their parents at their side. Both were probably 10 years old or so.

One was sitting outside with her mother, who seemed to be on the phone with doctors or insurance (story of our life). The little girl was sunken in to her wheelchair that could have fit about 2 more of her. She had dark hair and an NG tube that was hooked to some orange juice. I didn't see her move much as we walked up the sidewalk. It seemed like a huge task to remove her mask as we were about 100 feet away. She was probably coming out of treatments or something like that.

The other little girl was a little heavy set with blonde hair pulled back into a ponytail. I probably wouldn't have paid much attention to her except she was surrounded by about 10 people.

Family, sisters, and a couple nurses. As I got closer, I noticed her talking behind the mask, and her eyes were filled with tears. Her dad walked beside her as her mother pushed her wheelchair. I could tell something was going on, but in a way I didn't really want to know.

I only describe seeing these two girls because they will never leave my mind, ever.

The little girl outside about brought me to my knees first. It probably would have been better to say she looked more like a zombie or post-op patient than a little girl. She just had that look of "They woke me up. Now let me go back to sleep." As we got closer, I noticed her eyes. Sunken and dark don't begin to describe them. There looked like there was no life behind them. We got about 10 feet away and she sort of turned her head to P's pink stroller. We got closer, and as we were a couple feet away, she turned her head to look at Penelope. Almost instantly it went from this blank stare to a meaningful, genuine smile. Her eyes lit up; you could see her teeth from the grin. She never moved her body, just her eyes and mouth. We got right next to her, and she looked up at me with that smile. We kept walking and I noticed she went back to that look of just staring off into the distance as we got out of sight. I felt my knees

get weak immediately. I'm not talking about getting married knees

weak. I'm saying something came over me like never before. We

kept walking towards the entrance, and thank God I had my

sunglasses on because I'm sure I looked like a wreck. Those tears

came and went pretty fast because I knew I was about to walk inside

and would have to take my sunglasses off. I was about to pull a real

D-bag move and just wear them walking the halls. I wanted to keep

crying.

The other little girl, followed by her army of support about

took what strength I had left. P and Ellen were heading back to the

room while I dropped off her prescriptions at the pharmacy, so I was

already alone with my thoughts, which isn't good when walking those

halls. I'll skip everything that lead up to me hearing these words

because these things truthfully don't matter. **"I don't want to do**

this today. I'm scared and I don't want to wake up tomorrow

hurting. I can't do this anymore Daddy. I want to go

home." Those feelings you are having right now, imagining that little

girl being pushed by her Mommy and pleading to her Daddy,

multiply that by 1000, and that was me. I saw the pain in her eyes. I saw the fear. Her eyes above that mask showed what no Dad wanted to see when he looked at his daughter. I don't know what she was getting ready to do, but I wanted to do it for her. I wanted to walk with that dad and make sure he was ok. I also wanted to get the hell out of there before something else happened.

Those two little girls won't be the last ones I meet here, but they were the first. They gave me hope and sadness. They showed me compassion and fear. They also showed me how connected we all are here. I don't know if I will ever see them again, but if I do, I hope I can put a smile on my face for them. They need it. They deserve it.

I'M A DAD, I GOT THIS

I totally understand how the stigma of helpless dads got started. I totally get that in most situations, as in mine, the mom does most of the caretaking and hospital type duties in relationships and with children. I fully understand how a screaming child is seen being more comforted by their mom than dad. The rare zebra striped unicorn of a dad who knows what he is doing can be found, and I'm one of them.

Just maybe, I have this fucking situation under control. This morning I about lost it. Penelope has been having some immense pains, and there is no consoling her. It doesn't matter what you do; you just have to ride it out. Some last 5 minutes, some are 30, and some can be an hour long. This morning was a 30 minute(r). I had to go check in at 7:30, and she was whining, which most kids do early in the morning. It continued to get louder and louder as we got to registration. By the time they put the armband on her, it was a full out shitfest. I tried all our usual pacifiers, but nothing worked, so I knew I was in for a doozy. This part I'm ok with. Her screaming doesn't bother me much until about the 3-4 hour mark, and then it's time Daddy lays the law down about being quiet.

The part that gets me is every person there asking if everything is ok and offering suggestions to quiet her down like I can't handle it. I walked into the hallway and started making laps around the registration room so the ladies could at least check people in without P's wonderful high pitched scream. Four ladies walk past saying, "Oh, Dad, are you ok? Do you need help?" Then a lady from a desk literally 30 yards away yells and says, "Would it help to pick her up and soothe her?" I looked and said without hesitation, "You have got to be shitting me." Four more people asking by the time I got back to the room if I needed help or what I should do to help her about blew my lid.

I shouldn't get mad. Most dads can't walk this life. In less than two years I've gotten a crash course in nursing and can do a lot of things that most in nursing school haven't learned yet. I joke with one of our favorite nurses back home that she can just page Dr. McCall. The scary thing is I can probably deal with most stuff that happens.

I'm sorry that some really good people, some really good friends, turn out to be crappy dads. Sadly, it happens. It makes me want to choke them simply because it puts dads like me in situations like this morning. Poor pitiful dad with the screaming kid that won't stop. He must not be able to handle it. I don't say this or post it on Facebook to get people to tell me I'm a good dad. I'm doing what you are supposed to do. It is what Penelope deserves, and it is what she will get from me. If it is any less, then yeah, lady from 30 yards away, it might be time to help.

But maybe, just maybe, not all stereotypes are true. I'm a dad. I got this.

WAITING

We do a lot of waiting. Waiting on MRI's, waiting on meds, waiting on doctors. Hell, we even wait to get on the elevator an abnormally long amount of time around these places. Waiting does a lot of things for me, and really making me mad isn't one of them. I stopped getting mad in waiting rooms when I saw this one lady pitch a fit that was totally uncalled for. Right then, I figured it was best for us to just put on a smile and deal with whatever comes.

You get to do a lot of people watching, which has become a past time of mine it seems. I see a lot of people pick their noses, but I'm used to that teaching 2nd grade. Mostly people are glued to their screens, so I sit a lot of the time making up in my mind what they are looking at. I can't stand looking at my phone or something for more than 10 minutes in a waiting room. I don't see how people do it.

Fish tanks have been my recent calming method. I could sit and look at their big saltwater tanks all day. I don't know what is better: watching the fish or watching the kids come up to the glass and the looks on their faces. But don't tap on the glass kid; they don't like that shit. Didn't you see Nemo?

68

Pigtails & Steel

I'll tell you, though, sitting in waiting rooms around here, you meet some pretty interesting people if you aren't staring at your phone. Today, I met one of the private welders for the owner of Bass Pro shops in Missouri. He built the handrails in the one in Pigeon Forge, so you could say he's pretty important. The other day in the fitness room I met a Dad whose son's last hope is St. Jude's. He's been in hospitals for 18 months solid. Hell, I thought in and out for two years was rough, that guy looked about 55, and he was only 32.

All I really say is when you are sitting in a waiting room, just take a minute and don't get upset. I could get real pissed most of the time, but what is that going to help? I only write this one because I look at what goes on around me, and I don't want to forget the people who are waiting with me. They are part of my journey. To the dad waiting six hours for renal scans, to the mom passed out with her son in her arms, to the guy who's going to be his son's stem cell donor, I'm right there with you, and I appreciate you waiting patiently with me.

Pigtails & Steel

END OF THE WEEK

Most people look forward to Fridays. I never have because I love what I do and can look forward to most days. I think the people who live for Friday's have to hate their lives. You are wasting over 50% of your life doing something you don't enjoy. Sucks for you. This week I'm the total opposite. I don't want tomorrow to come.

Tomorrow is the day they lay it all out in front of us, and we have to make some decisions that ultimately will change our life. Penelope doesn't have many options, and the ones they have given us aren't exactly great. They don't have a chapter about this shit in the adulting handbook. If they did, it would be called "Shit you don't want to have to do" or "Hopefully you can skip this chapter."

We joke about adulting all the time. One of my good friends and I made some adult decisions about a car situation a few months ago with her dealership and my coaching staff trip. We kept looking around for an adult to make the decision, but there we were, all grown up and being bad ass adults. If only I could have stopped there and chalked that up for my bi-monthly adult decisions.

I usually don't get phased by much. My parents raised me to make decisions, see things through, and do what you have to do. My mom and dad were great examples of making things work, and, because of that, most decisions I have had to make have been easy for me. Tomorrow won't be easy. I'm more concerned with not losing my shit in front of all those doctors and being able to actually talk more than I am picking choice A or B. Or if you had Mr. Meyer's crazy ass for science in high school, you always knew 9 was D and 10 was C. If only it were that simple.

When I look back on this post one day, I'll know I haven't portrayed the anxiety that I have. This hasn't helped me be calm about a decision, but at least now I can say I have processed this part of the journey. It won't help me sleep, it won't keep me from crying, but I know I can do this. Hell, I have to. That's just part of life.

Nobody should have to make decisions like this, especially on a Friday.

PENELOPE'S PATH

This journey makes you feel like you are hiking in the middle of the woods. Alone with your thoughts, but surrounded by so much more. Every step you take might take you closer to the "end," but it also takes you farther away from what once was. My trail is a waxed tile floor accompanied by hundreds of other hikers making their way through their own personal Hell. My sky is filled with lights and tiles. All rectangles. All the same. To my left are people with their own terrible story. Instead of taking a break by the creek, they are sitting in wheelchairs and plastic wagons, waiting on the next breath of energy to make it to the next appointment. To my right are trees painted on the wall with the stupidest animal faces I've ever seen. Why is the lion the same height as that monkey with too long of arms? Somebody bought the wrong sticker pack and said, "Screw it, nobody looks at these anyways." Well, I do, Mr. Maintenance man; I have to. Every. Single. Day.

Elevators are like the one escape you get. When the door closes, you take a breath. For that few moments, you can just breathe, stare at the numbers, and not give a dang about what just happened. I don't know of anyone who really thinks hard in an elevator. You just enjoy the ride. When that door opens, it's like a whole new world again. Now this world still sucks, but it is at least a new part of the path for a few moments. There are still dads pulling wagons down the hall, nodding to each other with that sense of "Hey man, I know how it is." Everything around you, as happy as they try to make this shit show, reminds you that nothing about this journey will be enjoyable even on this floor. I'll give it to St. Jude's though. The aquariums and play centers they have going on are legit. At least waiting to get your next diagnosis is colorful and active. The setting of this journey isn't exactly hiking in Glacier National Park, but it could be worse. **This place could not exist.**

I saw this on a shirt for Infantile Spasms. It was pretty cool, and it leads me to my next thought- "I might not like the ride, but my tour guide is pretty awesome."

Pigtails & Steel

Before me is this little girl in pigtails smiling at her little turtle that my buddies bought her. She doesn't care where this path takes us; she has all she wants in her little world. She has us, her cartoons, and her few stuffed animals she loves. She looks up at me and still smiles to this day. No brain tumor, spinal tumor, nodules, or abnormalities can take her smile away. She doesn't see the pain and BS that this journey takes us through because that's all she knows. She doesn't know it isn't supposed to hurt or that you aren't supposed to get poked and prodded all the time. She screams in pain, but knows that her mom and dad will be there to do everything they can to take it away. She loves her grandparents because they are on this journey with her. Penelope hasn't had it easy, but that smile would tell you different.

This journey will make us stronger. It sure has beat the hell out of me in the process, but I know it is nothing compared to what my Sweet P endures daily in her little world. I have to learn from her. I need to be content with what is happening on this journey with me and just ride it out. I have my wife who helps take the pain away. I have this journal that lets me decompress. I have family and friends who are amazing and have gone far beyond what I could imagine. I need to sit and enjoy the moment like P does with her turtle and her cartoons. Yes, this sucks beyond comprehension, but it is life. It is my life, and I will not let it beat me down. Penelope has shown more strength in two years than I have my whole life. I have kids in the classroom who deserve my strength and kids on the football field who need life lessons along with their run plays. *I will be better and enjoy the moment. I didn't pick the wrong path. Penelope's Path picked me, and I have to keep on truckin. That's what she deserves.*

I CAN'T PROTECT HER FROM THIS

The Neuro-oncologist at St. Jude thoroughly explained her diagnosis, but I might as well been on freaking Mars. I was there but all I could do is look at Penelope in a way that I never have. This sickness isn't going away. As I watched the words "I can't cure this" roll out of his mouth, it took a part of my soul as it went in one ear and out the other. I heard him say it, but my brain was like Dikembe Mutombo in those commercials: "No, No, No....Not Today." I had to keep my composure to talk to him about our side and our thoughts, but inside I was done. I felt a bead of sweat roll down the side of my face as he talked about the MRI. I felt every single skin cell it touched hoping this wasn't some sort of hot flash that I was going to be drenched in. I felt my stomach turn and churn like that taffy machine in Gatlinburg that just pulls and turns, pulls and turns. My eyes were focused on the computer screen, but I was looking hours, days, and weeks ahead. I saw the tumors, but I saw our future too. I started breathing heavier and slower, or was it faster and lighter? Hell, it was probably both. All these feelings I just described hit me in about 45 seconds. I had to get my shit together though and the man inside of me said "Quit being a bitch and get this done." It was my turn to talk, and I felt like nothing wanted to come out. Again, something inside of me kicked in, and I said my spill. We made a decision, and we felt good about it. It all seemed so fast. He is an amazing man, and I don't think I could have handled it as well if it weren't for him, but that room in the back hall of E clinic has a part of me in it and always will.

A father is supposed to protect his daughter, and I can't do that. I have not failed at it, I just can't. Feeling helpless is what hurts the most. I can give her pain meds. I can keep her comfortable. I can whisper I love you in her ear all day. (Believe me, I do all those around the clock.) But I can't keep this cancer from growing and spreading until one day it takes over. I can't protect my little girl and that breaks my heart every time I look at her. I am used to being in control, and not having that control puts me in a mild panic attack about 47 times a day. Every time she cries I know it is a pain that I can't do anything about. Every time we move P, she cries. Every time I go to pick her up, it hurts her. You can't imagine the pain I have knowing just giving my little girl a hug makes her cry.

I can now process all this, and through writing I can at least get it out of my head, so I can fill it up again with more questions and concerns. I'm starting to do better though. Even in 24 hours my mind has started to be less sad and those voids have started to be filled with memories and the happy times. If I'm sad all the time, we will miss something. I wouldn't be able to forgive myself if I missed something, so screw being sad 24/7. My little girl needs me during those times. She can't have a sad dad. She needs a daddy who will take care of her and protect her as much as he can. That I'll do.

<u>ANGELS</u>

I teach for a living, so I see kids do some pretty incredible things. Usually, I stick to the funny stuff like my 2nd grade -isms I post on Facebook. Every now and then you see a kid in school do something that really touches your heart. Every now and then you see some little shit do something that makes you want to smack them. I don't care about the corporal punishment issue, but a good smack to the back of the head wouldn't hurt every now and then. Anyways, kids can show you some pretty amazing things if you would look up from that screen and pay attention. There is still good in this world, and as far as the last week goes, I've seen a lot of angels in the midst of all this. These kids here are walking angels. They might not have wings, glow, and float above us as we usually think. Instead they come with shaved heads, disabilities, wheelchairs, IV pumps, and masks. They all have one thing in common. Their souls shine through brighter than anything I've ever seen.

These kids see no disabilities. They see nothing but another kid. I see a wheelchair. They see a place they need to pull a chair up to sit next to them. I see a partly shaved head with a scar from brain surgery. They see that and compare theirs. I see a mask. They see a chance to look like Batman and wave at the kid next to them wearing the same one. They don't give two craps about what is going on. All they see is another kid going through what they are. It is the most unreal sight I have ever seen. The most awkward situation I have seen is where two kids just stared at each other because they didn't speak the same language. They looked at each other weird then just pointed to the game they wanted to play and started to play; the language didn't matter. These two boys were just happy to have someone to play with.

Another example that sticks out in my mind is a boy who walked in real slow, couldn't move his neck. Made me think of one of my "father figures" Mike, who can't move his neck like that either. (This kid might be stronger than him haha). This boy, about 12, had a bigger body, but his head was much smaller and you could tell he had major surgeries on it from the scars and such. I only describe

81

him because of what happened next. A little boy, probably 5, came skipping in the clinic all fast like most kids do. He got about three feet from this other boy who was struggling sitting down on his own. Instead of staring at him or watching like most young kids do, he waves at him and says "Hey!" and stops to sit next to him and play while he waits on his mom to check them in. He saw no disability. He saw somebody he wanted to talk to and looked nice to sit next to.

These kids have changed the way I look at all of this just by being children. They know the evil of this world- they are freaking living it- but they continue to do good. They don't judge. They say Hey! They don't walk the other way. They walk up to them. They don't stare. They talk. They don't scoot over hoping they don't sit next to them. They make room so they can. Now which one sounds like adults and which one sounds like what should be happening?

These kids don't want pity. They want somebody to play with. One day I'll read this and smile about all these little angels with their shaved heads, wheelchairs, and surgery scars. Most of them don't even get to go to school, but they have been teachers this whole time. Souls aren't disabled. Souls are forever free and just waiting

for someone to say Hey! They only become disabled when you treat

them that way.

MY LETTER TO CANCER

Dear Cancer,

First off, F you and all your different types. I've always seen you show up around me. My grandfather fell to you, and many family friends have battled you throughout my life. It wasn't until you invaded my precious little girl that I really started to hate you fully. I've always known you could destroy cells and take over people's body. There are a lot of other things I have learned about you while our family has been at St. Jude. So before I go any further, just know you are getting this letter from a dad who is stronger than he has ever been before, so when I say "I will fight", you better pack your lunch because I don't plan on ever giving up.

I will admit you scared the shit out of me at first. When I heard the word Cancer and my daughter in the same sentence, I cried. I cried for days because you made me feel helpless. I have always felt for those who you have invaded, but this was a different kind of feeling. What I didn't know is what I would learn from you. I learned how strong my 22 month 16 pound little girl is. Even though you took her legs from her, she still smiles, still loves Minnie

Mouse, and still enjoys doing things like going to the Zoo and seeing Graceland. You have taken one of her favorite things in kicking her legs, but she's still looking at her daddy with those beautiful eyes saying, "I'm ok. Let's go have fun. Screw this Cancer." I learned how strong my wife and I are together and that you might break us down at night, but when it comes to it, we don't even think about you and do what we have to with and for our little girl. I learned that through writing I can clear my head and not let you consume my thoughts. How you like them apples? You might be fighting against us and you might win one day, but you can't make us quit.

I learned that there are people like Dr. A., her Neuro-oncologist. I know for a fact if it wasn't for them being in our corner, we wouldn't be at the place in our hearts and minds that we are now. They fight you every day and have a pretty dang good record against you. They are amazing people and with their entire staff, will continue the fight for all these precious angels who come into E Clinic.

I learned the strength and grace of children like no other. You might make them wear masks outside to ward off infection; you might take a limb or even their hair. The one thing you can't take is their souls. I don't care what you do, but every kid sitting there is giving you the proverbial middle finger and fighting with more strength than you'll ever have.

I know you have learned some things from Penelope and her soldiers as well. You probably thought you could just sit in her brain and spine and take over without a fight. Yep, you are an idiot. She continues to do things you say she can't and will to the last day.

I bet you didn't think a community would surround our family with love and prayer to the point we cry out of happiness and our hearts being touched as much as we do sadness. Tshirts, profile pics, hashtags, the high school lights, and hundreds of messages have poured out over the past weeks to show support of anything that stands against you. Some people have never met Penelope, but have gained strength in their life through our fight. There have been more prayers sent to the Man above than you have cells. God's army is stronger than your army of cells any day. You might test my Faith, and truthfully you shook it pretty good. All I did for weeks was ask why? I still do, but knowing we have an army of people behind us praying will only get me through this. Get you some of that.

I bet you didn't think high school kids would turn against you like this. I bet you didn't think that teenagers, who are normally consumed with other things, would stop and band together for this little girl. Through prayers at ball fields and at home, they have come to realize the evil in this world should be met head on. They have put P's on wristbands, banners, helmets, gloves, tweets, statuses, and most importantly in their hearts. One of them one day might be affected by you, but they see the strength that it takes and will be ready for you.

We have a new normal that is a part of our daily lives thanks to you. You have taken a possible future away from us, but you can't take the present. You have made us more alive and in the moment than ever before. I notice everything now. I cherish every moment. People have come together for a cause, and that, in itself, has power. God has been present this whole time; we've just had to look for him and search for him. I don't believe everything happens for a reason, but this is our journey, and although we don't have to accept it, we can make the best out of it. When life gave us this lemon, we made orange juice and had you question how the hell did we just do that. I want you to go away forever, but I know there is still work to be done here at St. Jude's for that to happen. They will learn from my little girl and use that against you. Cancer, you will lose one day. I'm a mess inside and will be for a long time. I cry every day about something. I'm also Penelope's dad. That means Pigtails and steel will not let you take everything. We are too strong for that.

Sincerely not yours,

Andy McCall, better known as Sweet P's Dad

Pigtails & Steel

I DON'T KNOW WHAT TO SAY

"I don't know what to say" is usually a part of most conversations I have now. "I can't even imagine what you are going through" usually follows it. "I just want you to know I'm thinking and praying for you all" usually ends the message. People closest to me and those whom I've never met both use these phrases. My family even says it. Those words seem so redundant, and I'm sure when you type them, or say them you say in your head, "I bet he's heard this a million times, but I don't know what else to say."

I just want you to know that it is ok. It is enough. I don't want you to know what to say. I don't want you to imagine this. Knowing that you are thinking about us right now means more than you know. It is ok. I promise.

One of the best doctors in the world didn't know exactly what to say either, and he's the freaking man when it comes to these situations. All Dr. A was left with was "I can't cure this." So if the best in the world couldn't come up with anything more, I don't expect you to. These situations suck worse than anything. Nobody wants to see a child sick or hurting, especially a little one who has had

to fight their whole life. The English language, as complicated and

intricate as it is, doesn't have a magic combination of phrases made

for these situations. Cancer takes the words out of your mouth. It

has a funny way of taking a situation that seems like it needs words of

encouragement and leaves you speechless. Truthfully, as a dad in this

situation, I don't know what to say either. All I can tell Penelope is

that Daddy loves you. I can't say magic words to make her feel

better. I sure as hell can't sing a song that helps (that usually causes

more crying by anybody hearing it). I couldn't soothe her for two

weeks when I picked her up as she was screaming by saying softly

"It's ok baby, shhhh," so I can't even imagine someone seeing the

situation from the outside would have anything either. It is ok

though. Chalk up another F you to cancer for taking everything we

know we should say and leave it on the tip of our tongues.

I don't want you to imagine this happening to your family or

your little one. I don't wish this on my worst enemy. You don't

want to think about sitting in the back room of E Clinic to hear your

little pigtail princess has an incurable cancer that they don't know very much about. I don't want you to have to sit in front of an MRI to see these little white glowing masses, taking over your child's body, that you can't do anything about it. I don't want you to have to look at your baby every night, and when you kiss her forehead, wonder if this is the last time you will get to do this. I don't want you to have to make a bucket list of things you'll never get to do again. So now that we are both crying, STOP. I have to stop myself too. Life isn't about dying: it is about living. So instead of imagining that, just live. I can't imagine months or years anymore. I have to live and do it now. So that's why you shouldn't imagine. We take it hour by hour day by day. If all I did was imagine, I might miss out of on something. We just have to do better with what we have in front of us. Imagining doesn't get us anywhere. I can imagine a different life, but that's not going to help anybody. So it's ok. I promise. I don't want you to imagine this because it isn't going to get anybody anywhere.

I can honestly say that thinking of us, praying for us, or sending good vibes our way is enough. I know it doesn't seem like you are doing anything, but you are. I was talking to a dad about the different prayers at the football field, softball field, baseball field, and the countless prayer lists people have added us to. He said it best: "Damn, man, I couldn't imagine the strength that gives you to go through this junk." I started to think about it. I know we weren't there for those prayers, but I felt them. Seeing the pictures of them hit me straight in the heart. How could I give up or give in when all these people are behind us? The answer is I can't. It isn't about letting someone down. It is about showing them that there is power in people coming together as a community, as a team, or even as a family and showing that they care. I don't care what your religious affiliation is even if you believe in God. God didn't do this; and there is no "reason" for this to happen, but what has come from this is bigger than any one of us. That you can't deny. Dr. Dan, our preacher, prayed with us continually before we even knew what we were getting into. I listened to our friend, Mrs. G, pray for P in our makeshift bed at Le Bonheur Children's Hospital, one of the most beautiful prayers because I know it came straight from her heart to ours. My friends dad, Mr. R, gave us strength to go to St. Jude's with his prayer for us as a family. One of my high school coaches and his wife surprised us at St. Jude's on a night that I was really struggling. Instead of sitting there crying and feeling sorry, they gave me an hour of good stories and ended with a prayer that reminded me what was important. I don't know all the words that have been said either in prayer or in just simple thoughts about my little girl, but I can tell you they matter and mean more than anyone knows.

It is a very easy cop out to say, "Thank you. I appreciate it," but honestly, that's all I've got. I talked with a dad at St. Jude's from Indianapolis who was fighting for his last chance with his little boy. I asked him how he handled all the love and support. Well, after we talked for an hour, all we came up with is "Thank you, I appreciate it." Cancer took my words too. It kills me that I can't say more, but I am trying to figure out all this too. Those words come from my heart, and I promise if I had better ones I'd say them too. It really does mean a lot, and many times I get a message or call with no more than "I'm sorry bud. I'm thinking about you and am here for you." And that is really what I needed to keep going.

Pigtails & Steel

Cancer takes a lot from us. It will one day take my little girl. What it can't take is a community and family that has come together for a greater good. It can't take my fight and sure as hell won't make me quit. It might take our words from us, but what words it does leave us with are meaningful and matter. Sitting on a bench in the middle of St. Jude's can be a lonely place. Let's be real; sitting anywhere right now in this situation sucks. I can't get too down because somebody somewhere is thinking of us, and I promise that's enough, and it makes that moment ok.

FACEBOOK AND FUNDRAISERS

I'm the last person to ask for help on anything. You can ask the people I work with or my family. They get frustrated because they are some of the most caring people in the world, and when they ask, I just give them the "I'm ok. We will be fine." That's just how I have always been. My parents raised me to take care of my situation because they always did. You find a way to make it work and just do it. It isn't that I can't ask for help, I just don't. I've always been on the other side of these things. I've always been the one showing up to mow yards, take out the trash, put money in an envelope, or especially delivering Mama's food. My grandmother, Brit, would sign me up for the craziest shit you have ever heard of and pick me up in the van with no time for me even to ask "What am I doing now?" I always wondered why? Of course, I would have rather been riding my bike the next street over or playing basketball, but somebody needed help, and that's just what you did. Brit and my parents exposed me to all sorts of situations. At the time I didn't get it, but now I see the importance of what I was doing.

I never thought about being on this side of it all. Now that I am, I see it from a totally different perspective. The help that has just shown up or been done without asking for it is overwhelming, and I don't have enough time to thank each person for what it truly means to me. Sometimes, I don't even know who did it.

Facebook brings people out of the woodwork. Usually I mindlessly scroll through Facebook looking at stupid comments in local groups, who has baby Daddy drama, and my favorite Jason and James posts. I rarely give any attention in my life to what is on Facebook after I close the app. I really can't stand scrolling through there more than a couple times a day. Just ask Ellen. I usually make fun of her for looking at the same stupid stories and creeping comments for the 20th time that day. Lately that has changed. Facebook was originally made to connect people, and lately it has done more than connect, it has brought people together for a greater good. Through Penelope's Path, almost 52,000 people saw her story. That blows my mind. For even a split second, my little girl was on the minds of over 50,000 people. Over 1200 people changed

their profile pic to purple. Just for one little girl and one little family.

So now instead of mindlessly scrolling through Facebook, it gives me

a purpose and a reason. To hear I love you from someone in my

past, to hear that Sweet P is beautiful, to hear that they care helps me

stay sane. That 10 seconds it takes to write a status or a comment to

one of her posts brings 10 seconds that I can't be upset. So even if I

don't comment or respond, I promise you I see it. It might be at 2

a.m. when I can't sleep, but sometimes that's the best time.

Fundraisers are another story. What has been raised for my

family and for research has been overwhelming. Through Tshirts,

bracelets, and just simply donations have made one aspect of this life

we live, for lack of better words, better. I can't even begin to thank

those who have donated or worn a tshirt with Penelope's name on it.

It isn't just money. It isn't a number in an account or a cash register.

It is a plane ticket for a sister- in- law to come be with her sister and

niece because she is needed more than she knows. It is a hotel room

one block away from St. Jude's that an Aura and Pop can stay for a

couple nights and be close to a little girl who means more to them than anything. It is a meal that family can sit together and be happy in the moment over some pretty incredible barbeque. It isn't a check that goes into the bank, but a cup of Dip N Dots that P gets to try on a trip to the zoo with my childhood friends. It's part of a plan for a room at the beach for a night, so P can feel the ocean breeze, and her Mama can carry her into the ocean with a smile on her face while her Daddy takes blurry pictures because he is too in the moment to focus.

Your donation to a research project at St. Jude's is even more than that. It is a family's peace of mind that, somewhere behind those doors that say research, somebody is able to try to find a way to make not only their child better, but more after them. It is a room at the Tri Delta, Ronald McDonald, or Target house for their stay. It is a bed that, although isn't their own, is a place they don't have to worry about fixing while sitting in a waiting room.

I don't even know what amount or where it even all comes from. I don't even know some of the people who have changed a profile picture purple or sent a message. It isn't about that. One dollar is more than cents: it is part of a memory. One profile picture is more than just a few clicks, but part of a movement for healing and support. Thank you isn't enough. That is why we share her pictures, her adventures, her bucket list. That is why we share the bad news, the struggles, and the hurt. It is because we are all connected in this. When things like Facebook and fundraisers happen, don't see them as "likes" and dollars. Measure them in the ways we do: Memories and Opportunity.

MY FAVORITE THING

"Yaya and Zouk" at 7:30 a.m. Now that freaking theme song is stuck in my head all day. If you don't know it, don't learn it. I usually pay absolutely no attention to these, but P was stuck on it so I just started watching. Maybe it was P's way of saying, "Daddy you need to see this". "Yaya and Zouk" taught me about my favorite thing. My favorite thing is right now.

Yaya and Zouk went on an adventure this morning, and every time they did something new, it was Yaya's favorite thing. It started to piss me off that every 30 seconds she said, "This is my favorite place to be!" It wasn't until Zouk got mad too and said, "Not everything can be your favorite, you have to pick!" Then that little nugget of Sprout wisdom came through. She responded with, "It is my favorite because it is right now. I just enjoy being here with you; so it's my favorite. I don't have to like it all the same, but I treat it that way." BOOM

Well, thanks for making me think, you little weasel looking creatures. Now my friends think I'm going crazy watching Sprout for fun, but secretly it is on their TV right now too.

Is my favorite thing getting two meds ready and flushing P's central line before I even get my morning coffee? No, it sure as hell isn't. But is my favorite thing seeing that little face staring at me while I do it? Yes, it sure as hell is. Is my favorite thing having to feed my daughter through a G-tube and then frantically stopping it because I forgot to catheterize her? No, it actually sucks. Is my favorite thing playing with her belly and making her move her arms because it feels good. Yes, yes it is. Is my favorite thing laying on a couch not wide enough for me while my daughter can't get comfortable and rest because she has nerve pain? No, it actually makes me cry. But holding her hand the whole time and her squeezing my finger can't be compared to any feeling in the world.

We can live a very negative life if we choose. If I wrote everything a special needs parent has to do in a span of 24 hours, you'd probably agree it would be way easier to just say screw it and be pissed all the time. I have to find my favorite things and live off them. For me, it doesn't take away from any special moments to say that this is my favorite time. Right here and now is all I can ask for. This little slobbering, bubble blowing princess has showed me how happy you can be just living in the moment. That is all she knows. She doesn't care if she's doing the same thing other 2 year olds are doing. She is perfectly happy sitting in her bean bag, watching her cartoons with her daddy holding her hand. That's her favorite thing. It will also be her favorite thing when her mom blow dries her hair and gets her all prettied up later today. When her grandmother, Aura, takes her for a walk that will be her favorite thing for those two miles.

If life was more favorite things, I think we would all be a lot happier. I still cry, I still get mad and cuss, but that's part of it. I don't ask God why anymore, I don't think ahead, and I sure don't take anything for granted. Instead, I just ask for more favorite things, look for them now, and love every second of it.

THE DANCE

P and I danced in the rain today. There was no cell phone, no video camera, nothing to catch the moment. That doesn't matter. For those two minutes, no cell phone, no video camera, no nothing could have told you what was going on. I have no idea why I just walked out there. It just felt like the right thing to do, so we danced in the rain.

Penelope will never have the chance to actually dance. She already had low muscle tone, and it was a long shot, but cancer decided it would take that from her first. Her legs are pretty lifeless and just hang there. I don't get to put her feet on mine and dance through the kitchen. I don't get to do whatever new dance is on the radio with her and act a fool for Ellen to videotape and probably put on Snapchat or Facebook for all to see. I'll never get to dance with her at a party and laugh because I probably stepped on her toe or am embarrassing her in front of some boy she likes. Let's just stop there and say this pretty much sucks. All those things dads "don't want to do but secretly do," well, Cancer said, "F you dad, I'm going to take that from you."

Well, F you Cancer. You can't take that two minutes away from me. You can't take the song in my head that I was humming to her. You can't take the drops of rain hitting her cheek and making her rub her face on my shoulder. I was soaked, but let's be honest, I was crying enough to drown us both, so at least that masked my tears. The drops began to slow down, and the sun began to peek out over the trees, so I knew our moment was about over. We came inside and simply resumed our normal routine, which, yeah, included that damn Caillou.

Cancer took all those things from me, but it also gave me something more. It gave me two minutes of pure Daddy Daughter time. It gave me a memory that I'll have for the rest of my life. Whenever it rains, I'll smile. Hell, I'll probably cry a little too, but the rain will mask that again, so it won't matter. I don't have to dwell on what dances won't happen. I got to dance right now, and that's what matters in my life. Sure I'll be bitter when I pass out the flyers of the Daddy Daughter dances at school. I just only hope that when they do get to dance, they don't worry about updates on their cell phone or count the minutes until they can crack that well deserved beer afterwards. I hope they get to look down at their daughter and not even hear music over the moment. Cancer can't take all those moments; it isn't that powerful. We take away those moments from ourselves, and that is just as bad.

"SHE LOOKS SO GOOD?!"

Stage 4 medulloepithelioma cancer. Malignant tumors. Very aggressive. Weeks to months to live. Those are the highlights that many of you know about P. Now what does that look like? If you were like me, all I thought about was hospitals, ventilators, feeding tubes, grasping for breath, and crying…..a lot of crying. Penelope's diagnosis does not define her. It never has, and it never will. My little pigtail princess gives cancer a run for its money every single day.

My good friend Josh came by the other day and said something that really stuck with me: "I sat in the car and prepared myself for what I thought was near the end. I knew I had to be strong for you while I sat in here." We sort of looked at each other and he said, whether he remembers or not, "This isn't the cancer I was imagining." This is exactly what I needed to hear. In all this pain I carry in my heart from sun up to sun down, I forgot to notice something. I forgot to notice how P is dealing with cancer. I've been so blinded by how I am dealing with cancer that I haven't really looked at how she is dealing with this hell.

The thing is, this is cancer. This is what it should look like. Strength....Courage...Faith. She has more strength in that 17 pound body that I've ever thought about. She doesn't know it is courage, but she's fighting something she can't win, but it doesn't bother her. She has faith in all those around her. She has faith that can't be shaken. Preacher Ritchey said it best.: "This is where the rubber meets the road when it comes to faith. It is going to be shaken, bent, crushed, and everything in between. But it is ok. You will rise above that because she will." There's a lot of different things you can call it, I simply just call it Pigtails and Steel.

P knows nothing but to fight. She doesn't see it as fighting, but just simply living. Cancer took her legs, but she still will shake those pigtails like it is going out of style. She will still move her arms to the best of her ability. She will still Woo! cuter than Rick Flair ever hoped for. She will still smile ever so often because that's just what she does. She still looks at her mama when she brushes her teeth. She will still look me in the eye when I say "Daddy loves you" before she goes to sleep at night. It doesn't matter if it is in a hospital bed, an MRI waiting room, an ambulance, her bff Harper's boppy, or her favorite place the bean bag, Penelope just does what she wants when she wants. She lives to live, not lives to die.

I've learned to explain her cancer, but not dwell on it. I've learned to see things on the bucket list as her firsts, not her last. I don't mind questions about how she's doing. It gives me an opportunity to talk about her. I lost a piece of myself in all those hospital rooms and doctor's offices; that is just what happens. I have found myself when I walked out of them. Her diagnosis doesn't define her; it will also not define me. I am not the father of a sick girl. I am a father of Penelope. She will make her own definition, so I'll just keep writing until we figure out what that is.

GOOGLE SAYS SORRY, NO RESULTS FOUND

Surely, on Google there should be some sort of guideline and handbook for this stuff. Let me tell you, there isn't. I have looked. I even got so desperate and hit the 2nd and 3rd O at the bottom of the search page on Google. I will say, if you have never done that, I mean seriously who has, you should sometime because it is an adventure.

I've got 4,000 emotions running through my head, another 4,000 things I need to do, and 1 image of a little girl picking flowers that overpowers them all. I want to talk about believing, faith, addiction, cancer (yes, again F you cancer), friends, phone calls, church lady deviled eggs, and grieving. I want to talk about looking into Penelope's friends Josie and Harper's eyes and seeing my little girl. I want to, I have to, get all these emotions out somehow but I am not ready to let go. I can't hit that publish button because in a way I don't want you to come into this world. I talked about not wanting you to know what to say and that it is ok in one of my earlier posts. I really don't want you to enter this buzz saw I have going on in my head right now. Nobody should have to do this, but the truth is they do, and it is just part of life.

I go from crying about missing my little bit so much that I get sick, to smiling because she's here saying, "Daddy, it's ok." I get mad that I couldn't protect my little girl from something to being happy that a little girl touched so many lives. I spend time talking to P about what she's going to do today, then worry that when somebody comes over later if I'll even be able to sit there and talk to them. I get anxiety about walking out of the house, but feel calm when I feel the breeze because that was her favorite. This is all before I've even had my first cup of coffee. So see, in my best Ice Cube voice, "You don't want none of this."

I've written a lot, thought a lot, cried even more, and talked to my little girl a lot over the past few days. To all of you that have told me to keep writing, I have, and I will. It is just going to take some time to let it out. I wanted to say "Let it Go" right there, but if that Frozen song gets stuck in my head I will go crazy. I appreciate all of the love and support. I'm sorry I don't have anything more

than thank you, but then again, the handbook is blank.

TWO PARENTING RULES

-Enjoy the moment you are in. Dads are always thinking about 100

things at a time. I know I sure did. But are we really enjoying our

kids at that moment? Sure, you are at a baseball game with them, a

restaurant, or even just sitting on the couch, but are you really there?

Facebook and Twitter can wait, I promise. I don't get to do those

things anymore right now, but what I can do is remember all those

times and places I was with P and tell you every single detail because

I was in the moment, and, truthfully, it was awesome.

-Quit trying to make your kids "perfect." I was really bad at the first

of P's life focusing on all the stuff these kids were doing and P

couldn't. I wasn't mad at her, but it broke my heart for her. I failed

to notice for a long time all the pretty cool stuff she could do and

how special the things she did do were. I don't know your kid, but

stop freaking judging them and comparing them to everything else in

the world. Laugh at their silly way of doing something. Notice how

they look at something they love. Celebrate things they think are

113

cool, even if it is nerdy as all get out. I lived in the land of unicorns and Minnie Mouses. If I can find any part of that cool, you can too. And keep repeating that. Those are the things you will miss if you are sitting where I am. If I was sad all the time or didn't pay attention because it wasn't "perfect," I would have missed all these moments, and that is something I couldn't forgive myself for.

I'm not going on the road holding seminars saying these two things will make your life perfect. I'm also not going to limit these to just parenting. What about your husband or wife? This road we have been on can make or break relationships, and I'm pretty sure the statistics show it breaks more than makes. But I started enjoying these moments with not just P, but Ellen too. I stopped trying to worry about everything going perfectly and realized I'm 100% happy eating supper on the couch yelling at those idiots on Wheel of Fortune with her. Just be happy and enjoy the life you are living. When situations like mine occur, all you are going to do is second guess and woulda, shoulda, coulda, every single situation. The good thing is P taught me these things early, and my moments from then on were perfect.

Pigtails & Steel

TWO HEADED MONSTER

Grief and anxiety are a two-headed asshole. Just when you thought you beat one, the other one smacks the crap out of you from behind and starts the process all over. Today was a rough day. I won't lie. it was like getting hit repeatedly with a bag of hammers. Slightly worse than hanging out with a bored 6 yr old. I think today I perfected my fake smile, or maybe I just had this awkward look on my face in public. Come with me and take a ride in the day of a "Strong Dad" who is at the end of his rope and how you aren't going to fix it. Think about it like the youtube video of the kid who is on that stupid slingshot ride in Pigeon Forge and his seatbelt isn't all the way fastened.

Start the day with a good cry that you can't hold back. You try to at least make it through putting your contacts in, but one falls in the sink, and you know your day is going to be shit, and, trust me, it doesn't get better. Start crying again once you walk in the lonely living room that used to start your day with a kiss and an I love you. Now it is silent and a depressed cat just lays there looking at you.

At this moment you probably think, I wish I could just hug him. No, I have morning dragon breath, I've already been crying, and I haven't had coffee. Not a good time.

The next two hours are a blur. No TV, I couldn't tell you what I was looking at on Facebook or Twitter, so I resort to watching videos of P which just make the situation of the day 100 times worse. Cry #4 at this point. **Don't think some uplifting Facebook status is going to help. 99% of those quote things are stupid and not even correct, I'm a nerd, I've checked it before.**

Now you would think that your buddy coming over to hang out is a good thing, and for the most part is. In times like this people don't need to be alone, just FYI. Then again that's all I wanted. Enter head 2 of the monster: anxiety. I love my buddy to death, about as much as a grown man can love another grown man, and it had nothing to do with him. You could have inserted anyone here. But as soon as he pulls in the drive, my mind starts racing, I can't think straight, and I'm worried he's going to ask how am I. Well, then he actually walks in. Friends are good to have, and in my situation I have some dang good ones, but I still can barely sit still and talk to them; it just isn't in me. **Insert you wanting to come over and hang out to make me feel better. Truthfully, it is a good thing. But sometimes for me, like today, it would have put me over the edge, and I probably would have hid upstairs hoping you would leave.**

Going in public today was even worse. I was glad to see two people who gave Penelope a prayer quilt, and I could thank them. That felt good. Then grief comes back, and I never got to bring P there. Then anxiety smacks me in the back of the head when I realize I'm so anxious I don't want to sit there anymore. I have my wife and one of my best friends there, and I want to run out when they aren't looking, for real.

Spent the rest of the afternoon by myself. Glad to be alone, but interchange that monster every 30 minutes and staring at P's urn just talking to her. When I start answering myself then I'll worry. **thinking to yourself, I probably should have texted him today, etc. I would hit you with the "I'm fine. Thanks for asking" and go back to my little day of horror.**

Pigtails & Steel

The part that sucks is today I couldn't be there for Ellen. This grief process will not break us, but just like today it will bend us to a point where we yell and sit in different rooms. Not because we love each other less, but everybody grieves differently. You have to accept that and just ride it out. Tomorrow might be different, who knows. I could throw some cliché in there about take it day by day and all that, but that's not what I'm dealing with. I'm dealing with a loss that I'll have forever. This loss is something that took part of my soul with it and I have to figure out myself how to get it back. A grieving Dad doesn't want pills to make him sleep, he doesn't want to talk to somebody on a couch about how much life sucks. He doesn't want to go for rides or even walk outside really. I don't want to look at my wife crying and have nothing to give her for support. I don't want to snap because the water hose keeps kinking up and blow my lid outside yelling at a piece of rubber. I don't want to numb all these emotions because if I don't deal with it I won't make it.

Life would be better if I had something to make me sleep. I probably need a 3rd party to listen to this buzz saw in my head and help out. I need my friends to keep showing up just to talk and make me workout. I need random text messages and stupid animal videos. I need to get in the Jeep and just drive with my wife. I probably should get a new water hose reel. There's a lot of stuff grief and anxiety want to take away from you. They won't take my Sweet P's memory. They won't take all the fight and strength she gave me. They'll test it, but hey, day by day right?

SWEET P'S SERVICE

They don't have a chapter for this in a handbook anywhere, so I'll do the best I can. First, I just wanted to say thank you all for everything. Growing up you always did things like going to funerals, but you never pictured it from this side. All I can say is you don't want to be on this side, but if you have to be, words can't describe the feeling of support we have. Thank you really doesn't cover it all, but really that's all I have right now.

My little girl isn't hurting anymore and doesn't have to fight one more day. I want to be selfish and have her in my arms, but she's in God's arms right now; and I have to be ok with that. I know that she is up there in heaven playing with all those other little kids who don't have to fight anymore. I know she's looking down on her best friend Josie and taking care of her. But I still look to see if she is in her boppy or bean bag and I think to myself, "Andy, you are crazy. She hasn't stopped playing since the minute she found out she could." I know she is running and picking flowers because I've dreamed it and pictured it in my head a million times, so I know it has to be real. I struggled with faith and believing through all this, and I still do about every other five minutes, but when a doctor tells you "I don't know" or "I can't explain it" then that is where my faith and belief was. My faith is in purple hair, purple ribbons, and purple shirts. My faith is in high school kids and seeing that there is still good in this world. My faith is in friends driving hours from the coast, from different states, and those just across the mountain who have been there every step of the way.

P was so unique that there wasn't a definition for her. We just said that's P and knew she was going to keep going, so that's what we have to do. Ellen and I are the lucky ones. Penelope inspired all these people who never even met her, but we were the ones who got to say "Good Morning Time Baby" and "I love you" at night. No matter how bad it got, she always just looked up at us and let us know it was going to be ok. She spoke to us Thursday morning because she knew we needed that. She made sure we knew she loved us in her own little way. It was perfect.

I told P the afternoon she got her wings to never stop playing, and that I missed her, but I know she'll always be with me.

Coach B, from college, said something that was perfect to me. Sweet P is running, laughing, and playing non-stop. She finally gets to tell people how much she loved her mom and dad and how much she loved her unicorns and Minnie Minnie's. Her memory of this place will not be about politics, war, or crime, but it will be of love and of how much we loved her and how much she loved us. That's pretty dang good if you ask me.

The thing about all of this is Penelope is going to be ok. She's better than ok right now. We are the ones hurting and in pain. I won't ever be the same after all this; a piece of me went with her Thursday morning. I felt it. The pieces that are still here though are a whole lot better off because of her. We are all better people because of P. I just see it as our job not to let that ever be forgotten and use that the best we can, just like her. I love you little bit. Thanks for letting us be your mommy and daddy.

Pigtails & Steel

BREAKING BEANS

Breaking beans is one of those things you just grow up doing. I feel sorry for those who didn't get to do it growing up or don't do it when they are grown up. I would probably say half the people reading this are trying to figure out if they've ever done it or not, and those who haven't are probably going to google it later. Breaking beans isn't what it is all about. It's the time you spend doing it that matters- because for that time, nothing else does.

It's a time that I want to cry because I miss my little girl so much, but I don't for some odd reason. I start to say how much I miss her, but then I notice how perfect the little string that just pulled off the back of the bean is. I start to get the feeling in my gut about worrying again, and then I see how I just broke that oddly shaped green bean into a shape that looks like a football. About the time I finish that handful, the feeling of sadness comes back over me, but it quickly stops when that 97 year old hand reaches in the Food City bag and throws some more in my lap.

125

It's a time that you hear about how it is going to get easier from a woman who has buried her husband and almost all of her friends. It's a time she tells you stories about the "damn Cows" he left her and how many damn ears of corn she bought from this damn lady whose cow kept jumping the damn fence to get to her garden. It's a time where she says she's proud of you for getting up there and talking at your daughter's funeral, and doing it with what she calls a certain eloquence. It's a time that when all the beans are broke, the stories stop, the feelings are put into a pot, and they are cooked on low with some ham seasoning.

I never got to show P how to break beans, but I imagined her there stealing a bean and running off into the house to try and see what it tasted like. (Maybe that was a younger me, maybe I was under the bed, and maybe I left it there because it tasted like dirt.) She wasn't there to break the ends and snap it into big pieces, but she was there in the perfect curls of the string and the funny shapes. Penelope Claire was there in the stories, whether about her or told in some way that made it seem it was about her. Breaking beans could have been anything today and will be something else tomorrow, but

that's how you get through tough times: one handful at a time.

1ˢᵀ FATHER'S DAY WITHOUT P

Father's Day, another chance to say F you Cancer. You probably thought about it pretty hard before opening this one. You probably thought to yourself, "Nope, I know his day sucked, not going to read this one, keep scrolling."

I didn't wake up to breakfast in bed. I didn't wake up to handmade gifts on the counter. I didn't spend the day near the grille cooking for a big group. I didn't get to take selfies with my daughter doing something random to fill the afternoon. I didn't get to do any of those, nor will I ever get to with Penelope. But that's just life. It will be like this every holiday at some point or another for the rest of my life. Yeah, it sucks, but that's all I can let it do is just suck. I can't dwell on it, or I'll never enjoy anything else again. I will simply leave the negativity in one paragraph and a few sad moments I had today.

I did wake up to a letter Ellen wrote me from P and a text from Coach B that let me know I had the strength to get through this day just from his always perfect words. I did eat Pals cheddar rounds with my wife at 10a.m. I did take a Jeep ride to the mountains and sit in the peace of Horse Creek. Sitting in the creek, all those emotions and thoughts rushed through my head faster than the water was flowing. Then they just stopped. I pictured P playing in the water and just smiled. I did go hang out with Pop and talk about random things like usual. I did go eat with my crazy ass family and laugh at their stories. I did get texts from many of my friends saying thanks for showing me how to be a strong dad and great father. I wasn't forgotten on Father's Day, not that I thought I would be, but there's that struggle of "do I text him or not?" and that's ok, it's a weird situation and I get it. I did sit in the backyard with my dog and a beer and watch fireflies for an hour. Those moments didn't suck. I thought of Penelope in all those situations just as I did in the other paragraph. The positivity is what has to win, and that's what I choose.

I'll just end with this. What I did for Penelope in those 23 months could be seen as strong and a great father example, and I appreciate that with all my heart. I just saw it as doing what a father is supposed to do every day for his family. You are strong and make decisions. You show them love every second you can. You let them know how much they mean not just in some Instagram photo, but all those times that aren't "picture worthy." You watch dads like my fellow special needs dads, Logan and Matt, deal with situations and be proud of them for all they do. You learn from your dad and your closest mentors, and countless other men in your life and use that stuff to the best of your ability. You will make wrong decisions, you will mean well, and you will screw up. You will get mad, you will say things you will regret, and you will need time to yourself. That's all I did. I did the best I could and let the world know how proud I was to be Sweet P's daddy.

4ᵀᴴ AND 1

Life has to go on as much as I don't want it to sometimes. In a way, life sort of resumed this week. By life, I mean football and reading school emails. To say my mind is a combination of every natural disaster put together would be an understatement, but there are things that have to be done. School and football pay the bills, and bills have to be paid. The whistle still needs to be blown, plays still need to be called, and kids still need somebody to talk to. I look at it all though way differently now, especially after the first week back.

I needed football more than football needed me.

I work my tail off and would like to think that I'm a pretty decent coach. I'm replaceable though, and if I never came back, the game of football would never miss a beat. The Greene Devils would be just fine.

I only say that because going back to the fieldhouse was a difficult decision for me, more difficult than anyone knows or that I'll go into detail about. I can't look at the bleachers without seeing my little girl in her Mom's arms in the 3rd row, 2nd seat. I can't look in the corner of the endzone without picturing meeting them there after a game and getting to hold her. It's hard to stand on the sidelines without staring into the sky and wondering if she's watching everything that's going on. My sunglasses hide tears that I can play off as sweat because it is hotter than seven hells on that turf sometimes.

These kids don't know that though. They probably know I'm struggling a little bit. They probably get that I'm not the same as I was before. They haven't changed a bit. I still have to look at them flex on me because deep down they know I'm proud of their work even when I call them small. The big boys think twice about that 2nd sandwich because they know I've been there too. They still sit on my desk all nasty even though they know it pisses me off and just smile when I walk in the room and catch them. I still say "WTF" to myself about 50 times a day wondering what goes through their minds.

As I laid down to sleep last night though, I realized I needed that. I realized in some way, shape, or form they still needed me just a little. One kid said, "It's nice to have you back, Coach. I missed you out here." With that one sentence, I was ok again. I made the right decision.

You can change sweaty, smelly high school boys and a game into whatever you want when something like this happens. People lose children, parents, and friends every single day, but death is something that we will never master dealing with. It takes words from your mouth and turns your days into disasters. Losing someone you love more than life itself takes the joy and happiness out of your life in an instant. Their life is over, but yours must go on. You have to find joy again in something. I was lucky enough for it to find me on the 20 yard line. I needed football more than football would ever need me.

THE POWER OF NICE

With all this awful stuff happening in our country, it helps to focus on the complete opposite. I will stand by my thoughts of #yourlifematters because that's how I live my life and nobody can argue that. Instead of thinking black and white, I think about my college teammates and how we all bled Blue and Gold, no matter what we looked like on the outside. Instead of thinking about the idiots we have as politicians, I think about Jeremy Faison and what he did for the children of TN and just hope there are more like him out there. I see people killing cops, and I think of how proud I am of my friends Logan and Sweck and what they do on a daily basis. I see Pokémon Go players, and I still can't figure that crap out, so I have nothing for that. I've tried lately to focus on the power of nice instead this shitstorm we live in.

The only way I know how is to explain the power of nice is to give it a name, well, the initial J. J would shoot me if I said his name because he's not here to get praise for being a good person. Being nice is underrated these days. It is usually seen as a sign of weakness in men and faked by women. That's how screwed up we all are. We just can't be nice, period. There is this one person in my life, J, who by a few examples made my life better because who he is. I don't think J really cared about what people saw; instead he just wanted to be there and be a friend. J has sat on the couch and held P in a couple of the toughest times that there were. J called multiple times to just talk to me about 500 other things because he knew that's what was needed. J showed up to cry with me on the same couch that he once held Penelope. J took care of my family in ways that they don't know, and I'm pretty sure I don't know to the full extent.

J is just an example to me of what we should all try to do daily. If you think somebody needs something, take a minute out of your dang life and reach out to them. If you have the means to do something for somebody at any level, do it. Don't do it for some type of reward or recognition. Those people suck, and we all know who they are, and, yes, I've come across them in this life that we have been dealt. You laugh with people, you cry with them, and you genuinely have feelings for another human being and what they are going through. What I'm saying though is look at your friends and ask if you are taking care of each other? This world is going down the drain, and divisions are happening every day. The power of being nice won't reverse all this. I'm not an idiot. You don't have to seek out a certain cause or child, but just start with your friends. Your friends need you in more ways than you think. My friend Jason, one of the smartest and nicest human beings on this planet, (who also has a pretty incredible twin brother) said to me one time, "I'm happy that you are happy, and that's all I need." Not a bad way to think, ya know.

HOW TO GRIEVE

"Oh, grieving is a process. You'll have highs and lows."
"Grief shows its head in many ways. You will find a way to deal with
it." "Stay positive."

These are the things you hear as you begin to grieve. Here is
the truth: It isn't a process. It is now life as you know it. You have
mediums and pits of hell, the only high is medicinal at the beginning.
You don't deal, you see things in different ways. These many heads
are really just the five million things going through your head at
once. Screw positive: I'm just trying to stay sane.

I've grieved in the bottom of gin bottles. I've grieved
opening up the top of a pill bottle. I grieve reading passages of the
Bible while minutes later screaming "Why????" at the top of my lungs
from her bedroom. I grieve by loving my wife more than anything,
but also by getting mad at her about simple things. I've yelled until I

am hoarse, cried until I can't breathe, and thought so much my head hurts to the point of crying again. I've watched the phone go to voicemail days upon days. I've made more excuses on why I can't go somewhere than I ever have before. I've given to more charities and donated more change at 4-way stops than before too. I've said I am Ok and doing fine to the point I start to halfway believe it.

I could say a thousand more things about the past month and a half, but it all comes down to living day to day. One day is not like the other. One minute is not like the other. The only process I understand about grieving is this:

1) Nobody should ever tell you how to grieve. You do you and be okay with that.

2) You will become bitter with the people around you without even knowing.

3) Drinking an entire bottle of gin will probably make you pee the bed.

4) You need to take time to cry purposefully. Random things will make you cry, but you need to reminisce about the times that made you smile, even though you cry and want for them now.

5)   Don't give up on God. Your outlook will change. Your beliefs will be tested. You have to figure it out yourself. Nobody can do that for you.

HOW ARE YOU?

"How are you?" is probably one of the worst questions there is. For one I'm going to answer with "I'm fine" and smile, which are both a lie. The second thing is you really don't want to hear the real answer. Before I begin with the real answer though, I truthfully appreciate the people who ask "How are you?" and genuinely care. It really does help for that split second to lift my spirits, but, sorry, I must lie to your face.

So here's the truth:

I'm not fine. I'm the exact opposite of fine. I start my day usually crying for a few minutes because I have to walk by pictures and an urn instead of a snoring and drooling little girl. I don't want to get out of bed to pee much less go through another day. The last thing I want to do is interact with people and have conversations. I don't want to watch that kid suffer in class when I know their parents could give a crap about what they do. I don't even like working out

140

any more, but I have to because with depression comes eating, and I'd weigh 400 pounds if I didn't. I don't like picking up the phone when my friends call and usually stare at the screen until it goes to voicemail. I get mad at stuff around the house that doesn't even matter. I make my wife, the one person I can't go without, cry and not like me with stupid decisions and comments. I spent two hours of Thanksgiving laying in bed staring at Penelope's Bunny because I couldn't handle being around people and faking it anymore. I smile, laugh, and joke around while inside I'm trying not to throw up and holding back tears because something I'm doing is probably reminding me of P and I'm hoping that I can leave to go sit on the couch as soon as possible and hold her boppy. I look like I'm holding it together, but there's the truth: I'm not.

I don't want extra calls or texts. I probably won't pick it up any way. I am depressed, but I have to learn how to deal with it my way. I don't want to leave my house, but I do. I have an obligation to my kids to give them a great day, and I will do that, no matter what's wrong with me. So for those of you whom I do encounter during the day, I appreciate you and yeah, "I'm fine."

Pigtails & Steel

DEEP IN THE TIMELINE

June 9th wasn't that long ago, but it seems like forever because every day I wake up in the same hell as the day before. I made sure that during those last times I lived in the moment. I soaked up every single second that I could because I knew those seconds wouldn't last forever. I was wrong. I relive those seconds every single day at some point. I can tell you every single thing that happened from the time I got the call from Ellen to the second I felt all the breath leave her body onto my neck for the last time. The problem with all that is I'm not living in the moment now. I'm not even close to that and it took three minutes of scrolling through our local sports writer's pictures to make me realize that.

If you don't know him, then you are missing out. The stories he tells through his pictures are pretty much unbelievable, and his appreciation for a good beer is on the same level as mine. Long story short, I saw a picture I forgot about this morning and went scrolling through his timeline to find the original. Let's just say that took a while. In the process, I noticed pictures of things I was a part of that I had never seen before. I forgot about football games,

143

accomplishments, current events, and so much more. Timelines since June are almost nonexistent because I play the same one in my head over and over. I've missed out on so much more and cheated myself because I'm depressed and anxious about making it through the next hour and not living in that hour.

It isn't going to change any time soon, but damn, it about brought me to tears. I had no idea what some of those pictures were, and I was probably no more than 50 feet away from them in the background somewhere. Depression makes you live in the background. It takes away what is in front of you, and although you can mask it with a fake smile and "I'm fine," it doesn't change the fact that I won't remember this moment because I'm replaying the time Penelope held my hand all the way from Florida a few days before she passed away.

Live in the moment. Don't be in the background. It's a dark place that doesn't look the same for everyone. My background is in the middle of 1,000 people and a touchdown that I can't even remember. They say, "You live and you learn." I say, "You need to learn while you live," or it isn't living at all.

Pigtails & Steel

TO MY BOYS

This time of year, when the pads are put up and the stadium is bare, a coach really starts to examine the past year and if he did all he could. I'm not at the high school, so I feel even more detached than if I was walking the halls with them. The same boys I spent more time with than my wife haven't seen me in a couple weeks. I wish I could call or text every one of them every day, but other than they don't have time for that, I hope that what I've taught them doesn't require me to be there with them for it to come about. I'll pull a page out of Coach Brimer's book and just put it here. Maybe they'll read it...maybe they won't.

To my boys:

I promised you the first time you walked into that field house that I would never give up on you if you don't give up on me. When my daughter passed away this summer, I wanted to give up. I wasn't going to come back and coach this year. I was going to go back on my promise and leave you there on that field without me. You would have been just fine and probably never missed a beat. Something happened, though, that stuck with me and I couldn't shake. #16 looked me in the eye after P's service and asked me in his own way, "When you think you'll come back around?" From that moment on, along with Ellen telling me to go, I knew I had to be there.

You wore my daughter's initial on your helmet thanks to Coach Ballard. That meant more to me than I ever could truly tell you. My Thunder Gang got to see me cry before the 1st game because of it. I no longer get to see my little girl, but I got a reminder every day when I looked in your eyes that she was there. She would have been proud of you.

You didn't win every game and, yes, that sucks. The thing is in 10 years is that single game you lost going to matter more than all that we tried to instill in you? If it does, then we as coaches didn't get through to you. Football isn't life. It is part of life. What you learned in all those summer workouts, team meetings, HUDL studies, and halftime adjustments will transcend touchdowns and scoreboards. You are ahead in life because of the values you learned across Palmer Street. At some point in life, you will come across a situation that will take you to your knees, but I promise that you will stand back up. You will be able to handle what comes at you. It is in you. It might be buried deep, but so was that last 100 at 5 p.m. in 103 degree heat. Don't ever give up; I almost did, and I almost regretted a part of my life.

I'll always pick up the phone. I'll always be there to talk. I'm not a Hall of Fame coach, and I probably won't ever have my name on some plaque for some crazy record. I'm just Coach McCall who was never a hypocrite. I told you how it was whether you liked it or not. I kept it 100 with you all the time. You hated me, you hugged me, and you might even have learned something from me along the way. I'll always ask you how you are and if you have all A's in college because I care. Always tell your Mom you love her, don't waste an opportunity in front of you, and have fun. You will make bad decisions along the way; just don't let them define you. Don't let anyone define you. You do it on your terms, not someone else's.

Pigtails & Steel

NOTHING MORE WAS NEEDED...

I'm writing this one more for me, but maybe you'll get something out of it. I have a special kind of relationship with my grandmother. Mainly because she's cool as anybody I know or maybe it's because I'm her favorite.

Tonight will forever go down as a moment I'll never forget. Some know my grandmother Brit, some have heard the legends, some have heard me tell stories about her, and I promise whatever you have heard is true. In her 97 years, she has gained a lot of knowledge that I've tried to soak in over the years. No matter what you do though, she will always have a comment on it or tell you that you could have done it just a little different. If I'm 97, you best believe I'm going to tell you that you are an idiot and should have done it completely different. That's exactly what I expected to hear as she supervised my cooking of her Thanksgiving dressing recipe.

Sitting in her chair, looking at me from across the table, she took a deep breath and said, "I don't have to worry now. I think you've got it down pat." It didn't need more sage, it didn't need another cup of chicken stock and butter. It didn't need more celery or onions. It was right. The dressing was right, and it couldn't have been better in her eyes. Dressing seems like a trivial thing, but it is something that I have worked at doing well in her eyes. I finally did something of hers completely right; nothing more was needed.

The only thing I needed more of tonight was time with her. I've spent countless hours in that house through the years, and I realized tonight I hadn't always been listening. I learned with Penelope that you must live in the moment. I learned tonight that you must listen in the moment as well. I listened to how she's been solving the Cryptquip but can't do Soduko. I listened to her criticize Vanna White's hairdo and how she'd spend the $50 million Powerball if she won. We laughed, we talked about things going on, and just had some good times together. I hung on every word tonight for some reason. I couldn't think of anything better.

Pigtails & Steel

I hope that whatever you get to listen to this holiday weekend that you soak in and are 100% in the moment. Those stories you've heard 100 times will one day be gone. The people sitting there won't always be there. You've heard it 1,000 times I know, but did you really listen?

THE MISSING PRESENT

Her stocking hangs there in its spot next to her Mama's. Her pictures are on the mantle, the table, behind me, on my cell phone, and on the computer. Her boppy pillow is right under this computer as I type. Her Poppy cat is cuddled on her spot right above Tink on the couch. Her pink tree sits in the front room with all her ornaments just as they were last year. I moved her urn to the front of her special place, so the lights shine off the side if you look at it just right. The only thing missing is her. The piece of my heart that is hers is no longer there, but broken into tiny pieces all over my soul.

Yes, I'm depressed and have anxiety at some point every single day. Yes, I cry when I see all these cute things I could be buying her. Yes, I get pissed when I walk by a storefront that has something pretty that my baby would have looked cute in. I struggle constantly finding something to look forward to. I truthfully get upset when I have to look at others' family Christmas cards, and we don't have one. I get pissed when I think of all these people who will be opening presents and being ungrateful because it is the wrong size or color. I scroll as fast as I can on social media, so I don't have to look at the fun things you're doing with your kids. (Minus that creepy as hell Elf on the Shelf. You can keep that stupid thing to yourself.) I cry watching videos and looking at pictures because that is all I have left. I give fake smiles to people as I walk by because that's the best I've got.

All those things are what a dad goes through who's lost his little girl. There's a million other emotions and triggers that I have to navigate every day. Those feelings have also made me see the flip side of it. I don't get pissed at all those Minnie Mouses or fairies that fill my house. I stopped being mad at that "cute stuff" Ellen bought when I scroll through pics and see her wearing it. I smile at those Christmas cards the 2nd time I look at them because those families were there for us when we needed it and are pretty much our family too. I don't look forward to much, but I know that those 8 yr olds are looking forward to seeing me. I am grateful for neighbors who bring by a card, kids who hand me a gift card, and a young man that gave me a gift with his own words written in the inside cover. I'm more grateful for those little gestures than ever before. I'm happy for social media because it gives me an escape to share my feelings, read the ridiculous posts in our town's crazy Facebook group, and look at satire Instagram pages. Those same videos that make me cry also give me the strength to make it through the rest of the day.

I'm not getting into the Reason for the Season vs. Christmas trees and presents and how it should make me feel. I'm just trying to make it through a meal without having to go upstairs and be alone. My little angel fairy is celebrating her 1st Christmas without being sick or hurting. She gets to stare at all the Christmas lights, not just ours. She can be on a mountain in Montana or on the beach in Florida, but I know she'll be here with us on the couch. I truly want Christmas to come and go this year. I don't know any other way. I hope your Christmas is all you want it to be. Live in the moment, and listen in it too. There will be joy, and we will all smile at some point. It might just not come as easy as it has in the past.

MY LAST LETTER TO CANCER

Dear You,

I'm not even going to say your name because I've already given you enough time in my life. I wrote you on May 24th, but since that time I've learned to despise you even more. You took my little girl, but you also took a whole lot more. I'm only writing you this because it's time I lift you up off my chest and let you go back to whatever hell hole you crawled out of. This isn't about some New Year's resolution, I think those are ridiculous anyway. This is about letting you know what you took and what you won't ever have.

My little girl was my everything. You took a piece of my soul, and I watched it fade away as you left me helpless. You made me depressed and anxious from the time I woke up to the time I tried to fall asleep. I had to start taking pills just to get some type of sleep. Congrats on successfully screwing up my awake time and taking over my dreams. Asshole. Because of you, I don't always pick up the phone when my friends call, and I have to give the "I'm fine" line to people when they ask me how I am. You almost took coaching away from me. My gym time was few and far between. It was supposed to be an outlet for my hatred for you, but it only made it worse sometimes because I was weaker than a 12 yr old girl. I closed out my parents and made my wife want to hit me with a baseball bat. I didn't care if the sun came up, and the rain no longer made me think of our dance and smile. That's what you did to me, and that's what you do to most people, I'm sure.

You couldn't take away everything though. You actually gave me a lot. In your own crappy way, you opened my eyes to a place and the people of St. Jude. I've now seen God and his work first hand, and that is something most people never get. You made me thankful for friends who don't stop calling and don't stop showing me what true friends are. You gave me a renewed sense of purpose in coaching and, through a young man handing me a book a few days ago, made me realize that I am making a difference. You showed me what can be done when people come together as a community. I have a quilt made from some special girls who represent all the love our family has felt. I have a wife who, through our worst times, still loves me and puts up with my ups and downs. I have a tattoo that will make me forever remember what it means to be a dad and to never let her name be forgotten. You took a part of me that day in June, but you created a world around me that won't let me fail.

You took a lot and slammed many doors in my face. You took my sense of purpose in life. But hey, asshole, I'm still standing. I'm still a dad. I'm learning to live again, and Penelope's name is still just as strong as the day you got here. I still have a million pictures and videos (mainly thanks to Ellen) so all those good times will always be there. St. Jude's will never close its doors because that is a fight you will never win. There are too many parents, doctors, communities, donors, and, most importantly, kids that are stronger than you will ever think of being. You might win battles, but you won't win the war. I'm done with you and letting you ruin what's left of Andy McCall. I just can't take it anymore; so I won't. F you, Cancer, deuces.

Sincerely,

Penelope's Dad

Pigtails & Steel

RESOLUTIONS ARE OVERRATED

This time of year is all about looking back at 2016 and resolutions for 2017. I'll go on record now that this whole "New Year, New Me" is complete crap. Your phone calendar (let's be honest, you don't have a real one) changing from 12-31 to 1-1 isn't some breath of fresh air. It's going to be a difference in Saturday to Sunday, and that's about it. Resolutions to me are just words on a page. Most, and I say most, people don't have the mindset to pursue and conquer those things on their phone memo pad (let's be honest, you didn't write them in pen on paper).

Every day that passes is another day without my Sweet little girl. Time only brings me farther from the last day I held her, but another closer to when I can see her again. Isn't that a bitch? It is up to me what I do between those times. To hell with goals of losing weight and saving money. Life changes in an instant. I'll be more mindful of those things, but that's not what I need to focus on. Resolutions should be a mindset, not a single "thing" I believe. It will hit the fan at some point, and I'll eat that whole pizza, and the money will be gone, but it doesn't mean I've lost or it's time to give up. Cry in the bathroom, cuss for a few minutes, and keep on truckin'. That's all I know how to do. It doesn't fix the situation, but it does help to cuss after crying.

2016 was the worst year of my life to date. Losing Penelope will forever have changed me, mostly for the worse, I won't lie. I'm not going to look back much because I've visited that too many times in the past 24 hours internally and about 25 times through this blog. That's what brings me to 2017. A calendar year that I won't have P, but I will have a different mindset, and I hope that many of my friends do too. I can only think of three things that I think would serve as some type of hopes for a new year.

1) Make a Difference: I don't know exactly what I will make a difference in because if I set my sights on one thing, I'll miss 10 more. Maybe it will be helping fight for access to medical marijuana. Maybe it will be in one of my students or football players. Maybe it will be in this book I'm trying to write. Who knows, and at this point I don't really care. I just want to make a difference and make one of my biggest influences, Coach Brimer, proud. I don't know what those people in my life are planning to do, but it'd be nice for them

to make a difference too and maybe stop complaining so much on Facebook while they are at it.

2) Simplify my life: Too much of my time is scrolling through B.S. on Social Media, thinking about that same B.S. in my life, and flipping through useless channels watching something like Teen Mom with Ellen. (Teen Mom is a train wreck. Don't turn it on. You can't turn it off.) There are too many books to read, too much to see outside, and too little time to do it all in. I hope the people in my life will do the same. Less B.S. on Facebook will allow me more time to do these things. Hit the power button and enjoy something without a cord.

3) Learn to Smile Again: Depression hits you like a train and takes the fun out of pretty much everything. The other night playing Cards Against Humanity with some of my friends was the 1st time I've genuinely laughed and smiled until I couldn't stand it. I need to learn again how to do that. I'm sure I've missed things the past couple months that could have been a good time, but I just didn't have it in me. I hope that those around me do the same. Life sucks, and it will continue to suck if you don't do something about it. My friend and

fellow coach, Brigham, said it best: "If you don't like your situation,

do something about it. Quit bitching."

KIDS WILL MAKE YOU THINK

As a teacher, I see and hear all sorts of stuff. Half of it you wouldn't believe, the other half I have to replay in my head because I don't believe it. Kids say some of the weirdest shit you have ever heard, and I whisper "WTF" to myself more times than not. I almost have enough 2nd grade –isms to fill a small book, but today was different. It wasn't an –ism. It wasn't a laugh. It wasn't weird. It was a little girl looking at me asking 25 million questions that made me realize something- What I see in the mirror is not what they see.

"Hey, Mr. McCall. Did you get a haircut? Did you get a new watch? Is that a new picture of Penelope? Did you get your wife something nice? Did you forget to shave this morning? Are we going to do a lot of work? Will you tell us a story? I missed you, Mr. McCall. I couldn't wait to see you this morning." BAM!!! There it was.

She had no idea that it was a struggle to get out of bed and start the routine over again. She didn't know that I dreaded in a way trying to get myself going to not just teach, but be a good teacher. She didn't know that I cried a little when I kissed P's Beatrice bunny good bye this morning.

I realized right then that I needed to drop the sad act and be thankful for what I do. I was sad before, I'll be sad at some point after, but for these next few hours, I need to make her day worth it. She doesn't deserve a half-assed Mr. McCall. That's not what she or the other 16 yahoos I have need when they walk in the door. I might be the only bright spot in their day, and that bright spot doesn't need to be like the forest green a kid just stuck up their nose. It should be a bright yellow that the other one just ate. Everybody has a dark place, but to be the bright spot for someone has to lighten it a little.

A lot of people, myself included, let their situations cloud everything else. Bad stuff happens every day to every single person. We have to get our shit together and move on. It isn't moving away or forgetting. It is simply just needing these moments like that simple sentence to get us through to the next thing. The New Year

didn't bring much joy, but I have to look at it as new opportunities.

It is easier said than done; but I've said it so now I have to do it.

(2nd graders teach you this. They know when go back on your word

and use it against you very effectively...little a-holes.)

ELLEN, STOP TAKING PICTURES

That was probably the stupidest thing I could have said. As I laid down last night I spent, like usual, about 10 minutes looking at pictures and videos of Penelope. Pictures that I now have to hold onto forever because that is all I have. Thank the Lord she doesn't listen to me half the time and took all those pics. They are what get me through the day and are the only way I can ease myself to sleep sometimes.

Men don't want to take 100 pictures and videos of every little thing that happens in their child's life, but I promise that you should. For the most part, I just don't think it is in us to pose for all those pictures, but one day you'll look back and be glad you did. You'll be happy she took the picture of you two sitting on the couch, feeding her, reading to her, playing in the snow, set up the photo shoots with professional photographers, and all the other 1000 times you heard "Ok, smile!"

It really isn't about the actual picture, but all that the picture represents. You'll be sitting in bed one day and come across a picture you totally forgot about. You won't just see the matching

167

outfits (Gag Me). You will remember the hour it took to get ready and changing outfits 100 times, the slobber you are trying to cover up with your hand placement, the fart she let out as you picked her up, and then you'll be realizing how much you are actually smiling and appreciate your wife "making" you do that. They say a picture is worth 1000 words, but I think, more importantly, it is worth 1000 memories.

I hope that some reading this enjoy what those pictures represent and what they will mean down the road. But to be honest, I'm at a place now where I am jealous and angry along with happy at the same time at all those "photo opportunities" I get to see some having, but I soon forget that when I look at our walls and see Penelope in Montana, Glacier National Park, the TN Capitol, and, yes, even the hospital pictures. It doesn't matter where you are in the picture. It is helping keep those memories alive. That's all we can do. Take the picture and enjoy it. You'll see more than ink printed on paper, I promise you that.

Pigtails & Steel

SIT THIS ONE OUT...

Truthfully, it sucks to miss out on things. When you lose your little girl, you lose opportunities that you don't think about, but life smacks you in the face with them to remind you of all those emotions you try to hide. The Daddy Daughter dance is one of those that hit me hard this week. What hit me harder are those little girls that looked at me and said, "I'm not going," and I had to reply, "Well, I'm not either honey. We'll be ok. There will be more dances."

I cried as I turned my back to walk away from their table. I don't know if there will be any more dances. I don't know what the next hour holds much less a year from now. I want to yell, scream, complain, and yell some more about how life isn't fair and pisses me off. I want to be pissed that there are things like a Daddy Daughter dance and that I have to sit from afar and just watch it happen. I want so bad to put my fist through the noses of the dads who don't go and have the chance to. I want to cry because all I want in life is one dance with my little girl and knowing I'll never get it. I want to sit and be mad that something took her away and took these opportunities away from the both of us. I want to do all these things

over and over and just destroy something because I'm destroyed on

the inside.

But I can't. Not because I don't need to, but because I won't

let that side of me win. So, I just write about it and act like it will go

away.

People fight their own battles every day. Some wish they

could tell a relative one more time that they loved them. Some kids

grow up wishing they had a daddy to take them to things like a

dance. That's just how this life goes. It isn't fair, and we are allowed

to be mad about things. What we can't do is let it ruin those good

things. As much as it hurts, I still want to walk in my classroom and

let my little girls tell me about how dressed up they got and all about

their nails getting done. I want to hear it because it was taken away

from me, not them. I can be bitter all I want, but it isn't going to

change the fact that they had a great time, and it isn't my place to take

that away from them. The look in their eyes and excitement in their

voice reminds me of my Sweet P. It isn't about what could have

been, but what was and how lucky I was to be a part of it.

Pigtails & Steel

ALL TALK NO WALK

So many people these days want to bitch and complain about things. They want to rant and rave about how something isn't done right or something is wrong with the world that we live in today, but usually that's where it stops. ALL TALK NO WALK. People aren't passionate about very many things anymore. We have become complacent in things around us and are just ok with having an opinion. You have to fight in this life for what you want. Contrary to popular belief, life doesn't owe you anything; you have to earn it. Be passionate about something. Be passionate about anything, but just get off your keyboard and do something about it.

There are many friends I am honored to know who are passionate about something. Too many people want to complain about the life they are in but don't do a damn thing about it. I have friends who are fighting to help get people medical marijuana on the Capitol floor. I have a friend who left her job in order to continue the fight for research and awareness, so her precious baby girl can grow up in a better world. I have a wife who speaks out against ignorance and fought so hard for my baby girl that I felt at times I wasn't doing enough and made me work harder. I have friends from college who helped put books in hands of kids in inner city Charlotte. I got to do and be a part of so many things because of Penelope. I won't ask what you've done lately because chances are you are asking yourself.

I'm passionate about my kids learning and understanding the world around them, not just what some data says they should do. I teach them empathy through St. Jude's and open their eyes to what is outside of their little bubble in order to make that bubble bigger or even nonexistent. I preach to my football players about work ethic and drive. I walk the walk though. I read, I get better, I workout when I don't want to because if I don't then I'm just another person talking about something. As a teacher and a coach, I have a great platform to express my passions and pass them along to others. Everyone, no matter the road you've taken, has an opportunity. You just have to take it.

I'm just tired of people complaining all the time and not doing anything about the situation. I believe in another simple statement that I heard my man Brigham say.

"If you don't like your situation, get up and do something about it. That's on you." Simple as that.

THE BATTERIES DIED

Sleeping with a sleep sheep is probably not the most manly thing, but it is just one of those things that I will probably do the rest of my life. That few minutes of "Twinkle, Twinkle Little Star" sometimes is all that keeps me from losing my mind in that time where the real world takes me to dreams. Silence is your #1 enemy when you've lost a part of yourself. That silence is filled with that missing piece and everything that reminds you of them. Last night the batteries were dead, and, for a few minutes, I realized I probably wasn't going to get any sleep.

A few moments later, I noticed those voices no longer wanted to make me cry until I made myself tired. Those voices that usually keep me up until middle of the night put me to sleep. The pictures and the silence wasn't the enemy. The internal war with myself will never be won, but I'll take a few wins in the battle category though.

Taking something negative and turning it into something positive isn't really what I'm talking about. It's more about using all that love and energy that we poured into our little girl to keep fighting those battles so others don't have to. Book donations, St. Jude donations, medicinal marijuana advocates, rare disease awareness, and this blog have helped us all not dwell on the sadness, but the smiles. Helping others in turn helps yourself. It isn't about Facebook gratification, pictures in the paper, or everybody knowing your name for us and those families doing the same. It is all about doing what you can for the situation you are in. Her diagnosis was never her definition; our situation won't be ours either.

Life gave us a shitty situation. It all hasn't smelled like roses, but it doesn't have to leave us up the creek. We've got our paddle, and her name is Penelope. She kept us afloat before, and she will always steer us in the right direction. Batteries can be changed, and the sound we all fell asleep to will be there tonight. Another battle will come and another fight of the thoughts in my head will happen I'm sure. Maybe I'll let the whales or running water take my mind away from all the negative.......but who am I kidding. "Twinkle

Twinkle Little Star" will win...every time.

HOLDING HANDS

We have held hands through the best of times and the worst of times. I guess everybody has their thing, and other than butt touches I think that is ours.

We held hands during the IVF process, during doctor's visits, P's delivery, in the hospital rooms, at St. Jude, and during her final days. We held hands walking down the beach, walking down the aisle, walking through the woods, and walking up a snow covered mountain in Montana. We hold hands all the time, and it may be due to my long stride and her short legs we need to stay together, but nonetheless that's just us. She held my hand the other night on the drive back from dinner, and it was perfect.

There wasn't anything super special about it. We were just driving back on boring I81 listening to the Lumineers and needing nothing more than each other for a few minutes. I don't know why it was special, but it was. I didn't want to let go, and I didn't want the ride to end for some reason. Car rides aren't as exciting without P, but all the good times holding her hand rushed through my mind and just made me happy.

Penelope learned at a very young age that hand holding was our thing. One of the first pictures in the NICU is of all three of us, P holding our fingers, and the caption saying, "We will make it through this together." I held little bit's hand almost the entire ride back from the beach, shoulder pain and all, just to let her know we were going home, and it would be ok.

It may be Valentine's Day, and I might feel a little sentimental, but I believe in holding hands. It might not mean much at the time, but be there for your wife, your husband, your kid, or whoever. Just be there with them, hold their hand, and enjoy the moment of doing something together. Ten bucks says you are probably smiling when you are holding hands too, and that makes it that much better. One day, sadly, you might just miss something as simple as holding hands and just wish you could have one more time.

RARE DISEASE DAY

Rare Disease day is something that brings very mixed emotions. Somebody asked me if I knew it was Rare Disease Day, and I wanted to respond with,

"I lived rare disease for 23 months. I know what freaking day it is."

But I didn't, and just said "yes." I'm glad that there is awareness and a movement to bring research and funding to the rare disease community, but also it brings back all those memories of not knowing, living in a storm cloud, and moments of darkness standing in hospitals. Rare diseases will truthfully screw up your mind worse than anything will. The normal drill is you go to the doctor, and they tell you what's wrong. They give you information or something to fix it. You go back to your life.

Well, imagine multiple professionals in the field looking at you and saying, "I don't know. I can't fix this." FML right?

We live in an "instant gratification" world and that makes it 10x harder to deal. You expect your phone to work immediately, you expect your food in two minutes or less, and you will be damned if somebody puts you on hold. Now imagine that every day you wake up, every appointment you go to, you hope for answers. Then you walk out, and you have nothing. No reason why the seizures happened. No solid answer on why your precious little angel has to go through this hell. No timeline for anything, especially how long you have her. Now it probably seems ok to wait a few minutes for the lady to fix your hamburger, doesn't it?

I always said that Penelope's diagnosis was not her definition mainly because we didn't have a definition, and we had to make our own. She wasn't on this earth long, but it was long enough to open my eyes to what is important and what can wait. Rare disease day is much more than just acknowledging there are things in this world we don't fully understand. It is for the moms and dads crying every night because they can't help. It is for the kids going through unimaginable days. It is for the doctors who work tirelessly every day to help but sometimes have to say, "I don't know."

Maybe one day we won't have to recognize this. Today though, I'll just cry for a minute and keep on trucking.

THE RAIN ON THIS OLD ROOF

Rarely do we ever get time to just sit on the couch, drink some coffee, and listen to the rain on the roof. If you don't have a tin roof, then I do feel sorry for you. This morning though, it just seemed perfect to listen to the rain outside. Maybe it was our cable messing up that made me turn off the TV or that I'd already scrolled through my useless timelines and catching up on the world around me so I put my phone down. Nothing but me and the rain.

The rain is a lot like the world we live in today. It is unpredictable. Just as soon as it about lulls you to sleep, it comes just a little harder and wakes you up. Staring off through the window, you almost go to some dream world, then BAM! A little roll of thunder about makes you pee your pants. You try to make some sort of pattern out of it, but as soon as you do, it just frustrates you even more, and you realize there is no pattern nor will there ever be. I count the raindrops, but they change by the second. Nothing really

184

makes sense, but it makes perfect sense at the same time. Then all of a sudden the rain stops, and there is some kind of peace before the birds start chirping again. For those few seconds, it is perfect, then the neighbor's dog starts yapping, and the moment is gone, just like life.

Being an only child, I did stupid stuff to entertain myself sometimes. I would pick two raindrops and watch them race down the window, hoping to pick the right one or try to see how many other little drops it would pick up on the way like that old worm game on cell phones. I rarely ever picked the right rain drop because you can't predict something that you have no control over. It might run into a bigger drop and just stop, it might end up on the other side of the window pane from where it started. Just be like the rain drop. Who cares where you end up? Just enjoy the ride and pick up a few things on the way that might just make you better.

<u>JUST STOP</u>

You can't control a lot of things in life, but don't forget about the ones you can control.

Life can a complete cluster sometimes. Take mine for example. End of school, spring football practice, one year since our travels to St. Jude's, jacked up lower back and can't lift, grandmother not doing so hot, and 50 million other things I'm sure you can relate to. The problem with it all is in this life we forget to stop. We get so consumed in the externals we forget about the things that we can control. It is just as simple to stop and relax as it is to deal with all this stuff. "Oh that's easier said than done," is probably what you are thinking.

Most people resort to posting some sappy poor pitiful me post of Facebook and look to others to lift them up. That's the problem to me. We are looking elsewhere to lift ourselves and forget that looking inward is where the peace is. A hot tub overlooking the mountain is my current state, and it helps with this, but I had to make this happen. I have so much shit going on at home that I feel like I can't ever stop; but until I fix me, everything else isn't going to be worth it either.

Most of my inner depression and anxiety comes from the piece of my heart that is missing. Everybody has their problems and demons, but we too often bury them deeper and deeper because of the more "pressing issues" in front of us. There isn't anything more pressing than your sense of self and taking care of you and those you love. Ellen needed to be away this weekend, and truthfully, I needed it too.

Worrying about the dishes, the jungle I call a yard, the gutters that need cleaning, and the long list of financial issues that haunts us all every morning while brushing our teeth are no match for dealing with things like the emotions I see when I look at pictures of my princess and about throw up I get so upset. All I'm saying is just stop. Take a minute, an hour, a weekend and just work on yourself and the ones closest to you. Just like everything I write, one day I'll be drawn back to reading this and need this message; I just hope I'm

not too far gone to fix it.

TO MY LOVE ON MOTHER'S DAY

To my Love,

I could write a million things right now, but I know none of them will be enough. I've been right there the whole time. Sometimes holding your hand, sometimes looking in your eyes, and sometimes walking away because it's best for both of us. Nothing I could say on Mother's Day will ever bring back what you lost that morning. I only promise to never stop trying.

A mother is something you always wanted to be. I know that it is all you ever wanted. I know you lost that part of your soul, and although we don't know what the future will hold, I know that little piece that Sweet P created will never come back. I know how that feels. I know, Hun, that's what makes life so hard.

What you lost as a mother is what you also gained. You did more for your daughter in 23 months than some could ever imagine. Cleaning out blowouts, wiping up those damn bananas she'd spit out, and washing those bottles day in and day out was the easy part. That was just part of the job. That day you earned the title of Mommy was the day you started something that will never be forgotten. You did way more than what was published in newspapers and on TV. You showed what it meant to love someone more than anything in the world. You held back tears in times that needed you to be tough. You held onto her when she needed it the most. I will always say that she was a daddy's girl, but she was her mother's daughter through and through. Penelope was lucky to have you as her own, and she knew that. She told us that morning how much she loved us, but always you first.

All those signs we see are there to let us know how much she loves us and is watching over us. They are there because you look for them, and she knows that.

This day might not ever have the same meaning or be celebrated like it once was, but that's ok. It can be whatever you want it to be because you are Penelope's mom and always will be. No one or no thing can ever take that from you. I will celebrate it because I celebrate you and what you mean to me. I love you.

-Andy (with help from P)

JUST HAVE FAITH

Having faith is a process, not a phrase.

"Just Have Faith" is a phrase I hear a lot. This is what a lot of people use when they truly don't have anything else to say. Faith is the fallback when we can't explain something or are out of options. Faith should be anything but a fallback. It should be a stand on, lean on, start with, or anything better than a last resort I have so many questions when someone says this to me.

Have faith in what? Have faith in the same thing that made me whole and now leaves me broken?

Have faith in who? In myself? In God? In humanity? Two of these three have failed me on a consistent basis and the one makes me question the other two almost every second.

Have faith when? Just when I'm out of options? Just when I need help the most? Because this is the only time people seem to mention having faith. What if I started this venture with faith, and it is all been downhill? What do I do then?

I truly believe that my little girl is in heaven: perfectly healed and filled with love. I am more connected to my spiritual side and what I believe than some people who "HAVE" to go to church every Sunday morning. So don't get it twisted or say, "He's lost his way, and I'll pray for that." I pray sometimes that some people see blessings, even in hardships, and have something like I do to believe in.

These questions are just what come to my mind when somebody says have faith, and I don't think many who say it really understand what their faith is. Some have never had their faith tested, lost it, found themselves in the midst of it, and repeated that process every time they wake up and twice when they go to sleep.

I believe that everyone should have faith in something. It first has to be with yourself. You have to believe in yourself before you can believe in something or someone else. I've made my peace with God, and I am solid in my foundation of what I believe. My prayer for you is that you can say that too. If today was your day,

would you "Just Have Faith" or would it be more than that?

YEAH, IT IS HARD

That is the answer to everything this week. It's hard to think. It's hard to look at pictures. It's hard to wake up, and it is hard to go to sleep. I get so excited to scroll through my Facebook memories, but then end up almost getting sick to my stomach from the feeling of it being just a picture now. Life stopped a year ago at the end of this week. We go on and have really done some great things in her memory. That's what is hard and forever will be: the distance between memories of then and life now.

That whole cliché of time heals is complete crap. Time doesn't heal, it only takes me farther from the last time I got to look into her eyes. Time has done nothing for me but make me so mentally tired sometimes I can't stand it.

I've wanted to write a million things over the past few days. I've started and I've deleted. I've written a sentence and then my mind wanders 100 other places. Nobody and nothing can prepare you for the day you lost your little love. I have relived that day a million times, but something about the official "one year" hits you like a freight train right in the chest.

I wouldn't wish this feeling on my worst enemy. It is a feeling of being lost that you can't even describe. I want to talk about her, but I know I'm going to cry. I want to think about all the amazing things we got to do, but it makes me miss them that much more. I want to be happy with my friends about their little ones, but I feel empty inside when I can't hold her hand. I'm crying right now writing this, and I haven't even begun to talk about what I want to. That's life though right?

WHAT I SAW

Looking into Penelope's eyes was the most beautiful thing I have ever seen. It was a few months ago that I noticed something I had never seen before. I noticed it first in a picture from the beach. Something about her eyes looked different, and it took me forever to figure it out.

Those last few weeks I never saw once that Penelope was sick. I believe that it is God's gift to parents with special needs kids. I never saw the cancer taking over her body and slowing her down. I never saw it. I knew that she was tired and tired of getting poked with needles. I knew she was tired of medicine and needed rest. I watched it all, but I never once saw what she couldn't fight for much longer.

Those things never ran through my head when I looked in her eyes. I was lost in her soul. All she had to do was look me in the eyes and I was fine.

I saw strength not weakness from everything going on.

I saw a fighter that could have quit at any moment.

I saw myself in those beautiful eyes and it made me want to do better.

I saw hope that one day it would all be alright because she believed in me.

I saw a little girl who I wanted to give the whole world, but all she needed was what she was looking at.

I have to say that "I saw" instead of "I see" now. I regret spending time, whether it was seconds or minutes, looking at the things that were wrong some days. I see people all the time looking at their kids but not really seeing them. I see them on their phones instead of being connected with the little one in front of them. I'm over here wanting just one more minute, and they are wasting hours.

Pigtails & Steel

What do you see when you look at them? Do you see a disability or a miracle every day? Do you see their faults or their little victories?

I'm so glad I got to be in the moment for that period of time. My memories are now my moments, and I'm glad I had the chance to see the light in all the darkness. It was beautiful.

TO MY GIRL

To My Littlest Love,

It's been a year since I've gotten to hold your hand and tell you I loved you as I kissed your forehead. There isn't a day that goes by that I don't smile, laugh, cry, cuss, and all that in between. I miss you more than I thought I could ever miss anything in the world. A piece of my heart left that morning, and I'll never get it back.

But you know all this.

You are there when the sun rises over the trees in the backyard. You are there in those purple sunsets I see from the driveway. I feel you in the breeze sometimes. You are there when I look at your picture and even when I'm not. You are there when I want to quit. I hear your voice when I'm alone on the couch. It might be that I'm going crazy, but I know I hear it, and I feel you there, and it is all that gets me through the day sometimes.

I know you see my every move and everything that happens. I know sometimes you are happy and other times disappointed. I promise I'm trying to be the man you thought I was when you looked me in the eye. I fall short a lot, but I will do my best. I still can't sit on the couch without your boppy and can't leave the house for the night without taking Beatrice with me. They are my favorites, just like your pigtails.

I'll never understand why you had to go. I'll never understand why it was you who had to have cancer and everything else instead of me. I talk to God about it all the time; I still don't have an answer. You were here, Little Bit, for a reason and did more for your mommy and me and the people around you than I could have ever imagined to do. You were amazing while you were here. I'm just happy I was yours.

I will see you again one day, I promise. All those times I imagined us running through the backyard and having that real dance will come true. I love you, Sweet P.

Daddy

<u>Part 3</u>

These are my last few thoughts. Like you, I'm either asking myself what is next or running from what is next. I don't know exactly where this road will take all of us, but I know it won't take us back to where we were, no matter how much we hope for it. That's not all bad though. If I went back to where it all began, I would have never had a story to tell.

NEXT STEP

This is the part that I'm supposed to have all figured out on where to turn to next. What does one do after all this happens? What are you supposed to do after the one year mark? After the 2nd? The 5th? These are the questions nobody wants to answer but the ones all of us are looking for.

Truthfully, I have no idea. You've read what it was like to be in my head for the few months of diagnosis and the year after. Obviously, I handled it very well in public but came home to a head full of questions, tears, sleeping pills, medicinal cannabis, and one bottle of Gin that made me pee the bed.

I think, though, that it takes all this to fully grieve and work your way through the mess. There is no single answer, so we need to stop looking for it. There is no "moving on." You don't just move on from losing a part of your soul. You learn to live life like it is now.

I had to learn that my routine, as crazy as it was, will be no more, so I must find a new one. You don't have to abandon everything that reminds you of them. You have to just incorporate those memories a little differently and be OK with it. Life is moving on whether you like it or not. That is the part that sucks. It isn't that I like this new routine now. It is far from that, but I have to be OK with it because if I'm not I will end up at the funny farm painting pictures of flowers or something and eating pudding for the next year- without her pictures, her boppy, and her favorite spot.

I still cry a little bit every morning at some point. I have her picture on my mirror, and it is the first thing that I see clearly when I put my contacts in. Her staring at me with that mouth wide open in a big smile lets me know it is going to be ok. I don't get to kiss her forehead anymore, but instead I kiss her picture and ask her to be with me when I need it. Yes, this is in no way, shape, or form close to the real thing, but I have to be OK with it.

When I come home from work, I see 400 things that remind me of her, but instead of crying I make myself smile because those were the things she loved, and I love them too. I wish I could see her playing with them, but I can't, and I've got to be OK with it.

I don't sit in the chair without her boppy, and I sleep with her Beatrice Bunny. I never fall asleep without kissing her bunny and telling my angel I love her and good night. I'm sure some psychiatrist is judging me for this, but unless they've lost a part of their soul, they can sit in their chair and write whatever they want.

I live my life every day so that she would be proud. I go to work and give it the best I've got. I work out and do the most weight I can. I try to be the best husband for her mommy, but I fall short a lot at that. Maybe trying to make P proud is my next step. I mean I'm a guy putting his feelings on paper so that it might help another somewhere. Surely, she is proud of me for this one.

The next step for you might be anything. It could simply mean getting out of bed in the morning or facing your job for the first time. I don't know what it is, but I'm still searching for the answers too. I do know you have to drop a set, be a man, and take care of what is ahead of you. It is a choice to be the sad dad, but it is a choice to be the dad they would have been proud of too. You are not going to see the world the same, but it still has a lot of the things in it that make you smile.

Do yourself a favor. Whatever that next step or next thing you have to face is, do it with a smile. Your little one is there with you; they never left. Enjoy it and be happy while you are in the moment. Easier said than done right? Just do what I do and wait to cry when you get home. You'll be happy you didn't waste another minute. It isn't about forgetting them or doing things without them. It is all about taking that next step because I promise you that you would have if they were still here. You don't have to like it. Just be OK with it.

WHO DO YOU SAY THANK YOU TO?

One of the harder things to do is say thank you during all of this. It has nothing to do with not being grateful. It has to do with the fact that most of these situations make you feel powerless and less of a man. Somebody mows your yard, makes you supper, hands you some money, or calls to check on you. All those things you normally take care of have been done for you. Sure, being on this end is difficult and at first makes you feel little snips of your man card are being taken away, but just because you are on the receiving end doesn't make you any less of a man.

They don't know what you are going through, but they know you feel awkward. They know you are tired. The best they can do at the moment is hand you some meat and potatoes and walk away before you both start crying. Simply say thank you and give them a hug. You know damn well you'd be doing the same thing for your friends and probably do. It's what friends do. When you realize that all this is ok is when you truly appreciate it and what it means to be on this side. The lasagna tastes better, they didn't skip the weed eating, and paying that ungodly anesthesia bill doesn't make you as sick. Use that energy you would have had wrestling that dang weed eater string to work on yourself and your family. In the end, just remember who was there for you, because at some point they will need you too. I promise that.

You want to thank your wife more than anything. She is taking every one of these steps with you, some harder. She puts up with you when you shouldn't and doesn't get the credit she deserves. You don't tell her enough how much you love her, but you try.

You want to thank your mom and pop because you are a product of their raising and why you have made it as far as you have. There are no words for the financial, physical, and emotional burdens they have lived along with you. Thank you isn't simply enough, but sometimes it is all you have left.

You want to thank your in-laws because of all their support. They have been in the waiting rooms, the churches, the celebrations, and the living rooms when you needed a rest. You couldn't have done it without them either.

You have a hard time thanking friends who call nonstop. You never pick up, but they don't stop and try again the next day. You don't really want to talk to them, but you feel better afterwards every single time. They show up without being asked, and as much as you want to avoid them sometimes, you wouldn't have made it without them.

You want to thank your beer drinking buddies and their wives. They take you out for a beer and check on your wife in the process. They don't smother you, but they include you in everything whether you feel like doing it or not. It isn't because they have to; it is because they want to, and no matter how many times you cancel on them, they still show up and text you to do the next thing - like real friends do.

You want to thank your work family because you have spent a lot of time away from there, but they made sure you didn't have to worry about it. Your boss says things like, "I'll take care of it." Your teammates say things like, "We've got it covered, see you next week." Work is a necessary evil in hard times, but they make it better for you than you can say.

You want to thank your grandmother for giving you a place to get away. There is no place you'd rather be than right beside her listening to her stories. Sometimes sitting there saying nothing but the Jeopardy answers is all you need, and she knows that.

You want to thank a community that has done more for your family than you could ever imagine. A community became family and showed that no matter the circumstance or what's going on in the world, people can make a difference.

The trend here isn't about naming everyone, but making sure everyone knows how much they've meant to you. Just the part of being a man in today's society doesn't let us show how we really feel sometimes, but you have to get past that. I could go on naming people, but I would leave a million people out. The real people that do all these things for you don't need a thanks: they do it out of love. You need to make sure they know anyway, in your own way, however you want to do it.

For all those people who did something for us, from babies wearing a purple T-shirt to grandmas getting their hair dyed purple, I want to thank you. This journey a man goes through after losing his littlest love is hard, but you've made it a little easier. Dads out there don't know how to say thank you very well, so I'm going to do it for them.

THANK YOU.